just **W**RITE

just WRITE

THE ART OF PERSONAL CORRESPONDENCE

Molly O'Shaughnessy

Gibbs Smith, Publisher

TO ENRICH AND INSPIRE HUMANKIND

Salt Lake City | Charleston | Santa Fe | Santa Barbara

First Edition
12 11 10 09 08   5 4 3 2 1

Text © 2008 Molly K. O'Shaughnessy

Published by
Gibbs Smith, Publisher
P.O. Box 667
Layton, Utah 84041

Orders: 1.800.835.4993
www.gibbs-smith.com

Designed by Grace Cheong, Black Eye Design
Printed and bound in Canada

Library of Congress Cataloging-in-Publication Data

O'Shaughnessy, Molly K.
  Just write : the art of personal correspondence / Molly K.
O'Shaughnessy. — 1st ed.
      p. cm.
  ISBN-13: 978-1-4236-0261-3
  ISBN-10: 1-4236-0261-7
  1. Letter writing. 2. Interpersonal communication. I. Title.

PE1483.O824 2008
808.6—dc22
                                        2007032407

Every time I draw a line, I think of Mom:
... striking an item from my "To Do" list,
... filling the space after the pennies on the checks I write,
... dividing one entry from another in my journal,
... diagramming my complicated thoughts on a paper napkin.

And I am so very grateful for this—
Because I draw a lot of lines.
I think of Mom every day.

I'll never forget the day this connection was formed
in my little six-year-old mind.
I was drawing at our kitchen table,
The smell of dinner in the air.
She observed me from above and smiled down at me.
"Wow."
The word was long and drawn out,
Almost multisyllabic in barely contained amazement.
"You draw the nicest, straightest lines."

I was beaming, bursting with pride.
Mom thought I was really good at something.
How powerful her influence, how meaningful her praise.

Mom thinks I'm good.

Now that I'm older, I draw lines of a different kind.
Instead of using a pen and pencil (crayons are behind me)
Life asks me to draw more important lines.

And so again, every time I draw a line, I still think of Mom:
. . . drawing moral lines when the rhetorical
questions become real,
. . . establishing an ethical border when the rules don't apply,
. . . marking the boundary between myself and others
when it's not so clearly defined,
. . . sketching the lines that make me who I am when
I'm asked to lead by example.

Gradually, sometimes painfully, other times gracefully,
The lines are forming a picture.
And as I define myself, I see her there in the image
I'm tracing with every line I draw.
I am comforted and reassured, knowing that as long as I draw
"The nicest, straightest lines"
I'll be safe at home in the kitchen, no matter where I am.

Mom made it look simple.

I'm finding that it's not.
The lines aren't always easy to draw on my own.
So I trace Mom's footsteps. I sketch her profile.
I apply ink to memory.
I follow her path, stepping off every now and then,
Being true to myself when I need to.
She would want it that way.
And I stumble and I learn; I stray and I struggle.
I weep and I dance and I laugh and I sing.

And I've come to realize . . .
Strength and substance are drawn with simple straight lines,
Through carrying on day after day
With faith in sunrise,
Belief in truth,
Stock in what is real.

Mom's beauty lies in her calm,
Her elegance in the sureness of her step.
She is Serene and Resolved and Unafraid—
Somehow remaining Unaffected by it all.

How many times I've heard her say, "Life marches right on . . ."
So not many things really matter too much.
Continuance. Perseverance. Serenity. Straight lines . . .
The nicest, straightest lines.

Via Air Mail

Contents

What a wonderful thing is the mail, capable of conveying across continents a warm human handclasp.

Why write?

Whether scratched on the back of a grocery list, scribbled on a cocktail napkin, or etched into weathered parchment, the written word possesses strength of sentiment unlike any other form of communication. Committing words to paper is just that—a commitment in which we give that part of ourselves we deem worthy of a draft of ink. Both message and sender are delivered powerfully and often indelibly to the recipient. Written communication is the essence of human sincerity.

Who can resist the intrigue of a sealed envelope—that simple origami invention that carries the most genuine of overtures—punctuated with a colorful flash of postage stamp that guides it safely to its destination. The letter inside is on a journey, propelled by the eager soul who dares to reach out. Safely hidden behind a fragile gum seal (a privacy protected not quite so delicately by federal law), the letter inside gives a glimpse of that complicated and mysterious entity we all seek to understand: *the human relationship*. And for the one who at last slices open its paper armor, the key to this rapport awaits, as does a palpable energy that can connect two people distanced by the breadth of an ocean or by a mere tangle of bedsheets.

The words in a handwritten letter, like the two people they connect, are carefully linked together in loops and whirls, building an intimacy that goes beyond mere speech. Such correspondence overcomes the reality of circumstance or the distance of a world; it survives the passing of time and the destruction of war. And laced subtly between the lines, emotions resonate as quietly as a sacred message delivered in whispered tones.

However intimate the message, it is not always sweet. Like an arrow sprung from the bow, the written word can serve to unite or sever author and recipient, holding within it the satisfying nourishment of forgiveness or the cutting finality of good-bye. The pen can indeed deal a mightier blow than the sword. And sometimes we aren't privileged to know the distant ripplings of our messages.

This book is for anyone interested in the part that written communication plays in relationships. In it you will find

"Quietly touching one heart . . . reaching out to ends further than we would ever know, leaving all of us a little richer than we were before."

—Steven Gottlieb

simple ways to enrich and deepen intimacy, thereby building more satisfying rapport. You do not have to be a writer per se, just a simple soul with something to say. The chapters that follow will help those of us who feel tongue-tied to find the "write" words and, perhaps, to escape isolation and to find a deeper understanding of ourselves and others—soothing the powerful longing we often feel yet cannot name.

"Behind the need to communicate is the need to share. Behind the need to share is the need to understand."

—Leo Rosten

A DYING ART?

In this era in which the proliferation of the personal computer has wrought major changes throughout our society, nowhere are its effects more apparent than in the forms of communication that have become ubiquitous. Since its inception, e-mail has rapidly overtaken "snail mail" as the preferred mode of communication in our world. Certainly the convenience and speed of e-mail cannot be denied. Younger generations have readily embraced its rapid delivery and its potential for instant response. But if you have trouble deciphering cyberspeak, you might ask yourself, can we really *emote* via emoticons, SHOUT with capital letters, or indeed express any semblance of sincere sentiment via an electronic language that marches digitally across the angular chill of a computer screen? I think not. Evidence is mounting that although e-mail is an undeniable presence in today's world, its effectiveness is limited when clear and meaningful expression is the desired goal. Just ask the woman who was fired from her job for "illicit e-mailing" on company time what safety there lies in cyberland.

Since we human beings are social animals, we need other people to survive and to thrive. It is a fundamental part of our nature to want to reach out to others in the spirit of give-and-take. So it is ironic that although the Internet has revolutionized communication, bringing disparate worlds crashing together with the thrill of a modern big bang, it has also served to distance us from those closest to us. Our penchant for this new instant form of sending messages has diminished our potential to connect. My friend Anne lazily sends instant messages from her bedroom—to her husband down the hall:

did u feed dog?

Our reliance on this peculiarly contemporary sort of efficiency has other costs as well. The result of this newly implanted social distance? Isolation has become an epidemic. We find ourselves feeling locked up in the very modern home office we so carefully crafted. And behind our placid exterior, a "virtual veneer," there is submerged anger and frustration, leaving many confused as to its cause. The ailment is simple, really: we are lonely. But we need not be.

In this age when many of us seek to erase an ever-increasing hunger for intimacy, we need a solution—a simple way to reconnect with those we care most about. Letter writing, an art form once considered the norm, can be a

C,

Whassup? Me—Nada. BTW, your msg made me LOL. Did you get my IM last pm? Rock on. Doh! BRB. it's da man. C ya! :-(

Although willingly seduced by the convenience and rapid-fire speed of e-mail communication, when I compare it to the virtues of the handwritten letter, I gain little pleasure knowing that my IM (instant message) caused the reader to LOL (laugh out loud). But however you look at it, e-mail is here to stay. It is for us to decide its proper role when mingled with intimacy and information.

rewarding way to address this need, thereby rekindling the possibility of a rich and satisfying tradition of companionship. Current technology—no matter how prolific—cannot supplant the tried-and-true methods of the past. Today, in a handy and prescient reversal, the status of the handwritten note has been enhanced, taking on an even greater value because it is rare, more personal, and more meaningful, and is thus appreciated as a gift more than ever.

And before you speak . . . before you say that you don't have time or that you're too busy, remember: *we're all too busy!* But ask yourself what really means the most to you: Productivity or pleasure? Efficiency or experience? Existence or living? Emotions or emoticons?

I thought so . . .

Our task, then, is to unscramble our scrambled thoughts and put them on paper without the time taken by our quill-dipping forefathers and their ink pots. If this is your quest, keep reading. If you have a strong desire to reach out, I believe the proper channel for written communication will unfold; whether it's a few carefully chosen words dashed on a postcard or a romantic missive so overflowing that its prose spills joyfully into the margins, the sentiment is the same.

"Letters are useful as a means of expressing the ideal self. . . . In letters we can reform without practice, beg without humiliation, snip and shape embarrassing experiences to the measure of our own desires."

—Elizabeth Hardwick

LIFE INSIGHT

In this age of fantasy and denial, exaggerated images, and unrealistic expectations—all at breakneck speed—the human psyche craves simplicity, a comfortable tempo, and a grounding in what is real. We rush around in the chaos of our daily round, desensitized to snippets of international news; yet in our quieter moments, we thirst for a circumstance we can actually *relate to* with a small nod of the head instead of the shocking tidbit that sends us, mouth-gaping and marveling, into the realm of the bug-eyed yet reticent believer.

Despite our channel-locking, pop-up blocking, antivirus society, we are unwittingly exposed to modern extremism every day. It is truly exhausting. There is an enormous and uncomfortable gap between what we see on life's constantly

January 17, 2006

Where have I been lately? If Confusion were a place, that'd be my answer. I just woke up feeling overwhelmed and the day hasn't even begun. It's 5 in the morning and already I'm anxious about today's meeting and a blind date 14 hours from now! I want to crawl back under the covers and just sleep until it's night again. What's going on with me?

changing TV screen and who we really are. And in a world
deeply suffering from isolation, we have become increasingly
voyeuristic. Naturally, our loneliness has driven us to an
intense curiosity about the human condition. This pursuit,
however understandable, can unwittingly expose us to the
real-time media of "reality" TV, which *pretends* to dictate
what is attractive, acceptable, satisfying, and even "normal."
But most of us will never be asked to eat live spiders, choose
a lifelong mate in an hour, or crawl through a twenty-yard
pipe of raw sewage (otherwise known to some of us as
"dating"). We are too busy wiping the nose of a child, dealing
with dandruff, and paying our bills. Life is happening all
around us, but what do we know about ourselves?

First, you must trust yourself to discover your own opinions
through FEELINGS and INSTINCT. Easier said than done. In
our unrelenting exposure to what is extreme, we have learned
to prefer watching *other* people live. Sadly, we have come to
consider our lives utterly dull when compared to the Internet
headlines that burn their images on our eyeballs. But have
we ever really considered how remarkable our personal
experiences truly are?

The simple action of placing pen on paper, without
preconceived notions or grand goals of poignancy, very often
reveals important truths that enlighten us more than we
thought possible.

What are you waiting for? Get to know yourself on paper.
Begin by taking down some quick notes on what is running
through your head, rather than standing in the checkout line

Recording life's insanities is to uncover its mysteries.

Writing in a journal encourages us to encounter our daily lives in a mirror of paper, revealing our thoughts and experiences to us in a real and concrete way without the scrutiny of ridiculous celebrity comparisons and sensationalistic expectations of what "should" consist of life. After all, isn't that a *personal* decision?

and looking at magazine covers to tell you what's going on in your life.

Here are a few guidelines that will help you get started on the gentle journey of self-discovery. Remember: you are not writing a "memoir" for publication. Your journal is *for* you, *about* you. And if it's written *by* you, it's significant *to* you. Trust your instincts and get started.

+ *Start small and cheap*
  Alleviate the unnecessary pressure of a leather-bound beauty and buy an inexpensive spiral notebook. If truly pressed for time, take notes in your day-timer.

+ *Dear Nobody*
  Journal writing is not letter writing; there is no "to" and "from." No one is watching over your shoulder; you can be rigorously honest.

+ *Be unabashedly messy*
  Capture the necessary self-acceptance and release an essential childlike creativity by leaving perfectionism on the shelf. (No erasing truths you'd rather conceal.)

"Your life story would not make a good book. Don't even try."

—Fran Lebowitz

* *Spill it*
  Ugly little details are essential. Admit that you have
  negative feelings, that you have undesirable desires.
  This is your opportunity to be real.

* *List maker*
  Instead of attempting flowing and articulate prose,
  start by making short lists under a specific topic.

EXAMPLES	OTHER OPTIONS
• Gratitude list	• My dream mate attribute list
• Resentment list	• 100 favorite things about me list
• Pet peeve list	• How I'm different than mom list
• Things I'd like to change about my life list	• People who dress so terrible in church that it's distracting list
• Any pro and con list	
• Things I fear list	

Still intimidated? Remember these tidbits:

* As I tell my students at the local studio where I
  teach hatha yoga, "No judgment, no competition,
  no expectations. Just be present." Just write!

"Being entirely honest with oneself is good exercise."

—Sigmund Freud

- When writing in a journal, you need not worry about the complications inherent in involving another person. So go solo. You are alone in your pursuit of self-discovery, safe from the risks of revelation, and yet utterly exposed—in private. How tantalizing.

- Journaling is a path to self-soothing, so think of yourself as a soul healer, not a storyteller. Talk about cheap therapy!

One of the joys of journal writing is rereading past entries. You might not believe what you'll find. At times I look back and wonder if a mischievous little elf has stolen my diary and passed it around between my multiple personalities. Sometimes I'm an enlightened guru, other times a frightened child. Sometimes my entries reveal someone who is selfish and small-minded and stuck in her pain. Other times I am brilliant and funny and alive. It's an amazing and insightful

"You begin to wonder . . . Are your friends going home after a party and writing about you? I hope so . . . "

—William Norwich

look at the different sides of a human being. Something to be relished in wonder, though perhaps not necessarily understood. I use my journal to remind me of where I've been, to comfort myself by remembering that "this too shall pass"—just like it did the last time, and the time before, and the time before that. I gain a better understanding of who I am, who I am becoming, and who I hope to be one day.

However you might view a blank page, whether as an opportunity to share your soul on paper or simply to take note of feelings, frustrations, tiny epiphanies, and joyful revelations, think of it as exercise. There is merit in simply trying. The private diary is a place of **SOLACE AND SECURITY**, where we can revel in the self and its need to be heard.

And gradually, subtly, gently, but surely, you'll begin to feel the multitude of benefits as you stretch the muscles of your very being.

"Writing a journal implies that one has ceased to think of the future and has decided to live wholly in the present. It is an announcement to fate that you expect nothing more. . . . Writing a journal means facing an ocean you are afraid to swim across, and deciding to drink it drop by drop."

—George Sand

STRESS DECOMPRESS

We've all been through the wringer at one point or another in our lives. None of us is protected from pain. We've been made fun of, alienated, talked about, laughed at, cheated on, lied to, harassed, and fired. We've had our toes stepped on, our egos crushed, our hearts broken, and our dreams shattered. It seems that life's curveballs are unavoidable. And, unfortunately, we've found no safe way to prevent the inevitable black eye. If we walk on two legs, we naturally react to situations with feelings and emotions. Question is—*what do we do about them*?

Many of us let our pain and resentment build into angry tsunamis of emotion that swirl dangerously beneath the surface, just waiting for the offhand but insensitive remark or the "no cell phone zone" to release our pent-up fury on an innocent Starbucks barista. Others are so blinded by emotion that they don't know how to react. So they just lie down mutely and try to numb out on TV and ice cream while letting voice mail pick up. They ignore the emotional signals and pretend everything is fine. Just fine: "I SAID I'm FINE!"

Or maybe we've actually learned through experience how to manage our feelings of shame, hurt, embarrassment, and fear. We know how to accept rejection. We don't take things

"A writer is someone who spends years patiently trying to discover the second being inside him, and the world that makes him who he is."

—Orhan Pamuk

"It's not a bad idea to get in the habit of writing down one's thoughts. It saves one having to bother anyone else with them."

—Isabel Colegate

personally. We accept disappointment with diplomacy. Instead, we address the issue calmly and rationally, owning up to the part we played, chalking it up to life with a coy shrug, and moving gracefully on. Perhaps such enlightened individuals do exist, though I've yet to meet one who is sober.

No matter how we react to life's inherent doozies, an important part of the healing process is to use each painful experience to grow. We can learn to understand our highly charged reactions, try more adult ways of coping with life, and, finally, begin to live as grown-ups. And by chronicling our misadventures as suggested in this chapter, we can begin to see that there is enrichment in disappointment, adventure in the unexpected, and enlightenment in the face of life's next big wallop. After all, we can't avoid it (while staying true to the Self), so if we are to survive and even thrive, we must learn to repair the damage. It seems they just don't make Band-Aids quite big enough.

In your journal, you can express your emotions, exploding on paper instead of in public. It's a small step, a first step, a tiny bit of harmless action you can take when you're utterly dazed, confused, and reeling from a recent knock on the head.

Your journal may take the form of a simple documentary— a statement about what happened from your point of view. As you write, you may reveal questions that need to be explored in order to find closure. You may begin to see the part you played and consider taking responsibility, or you may come up with a vast collection of brilliant things you might have said if only given the time. Yet another possibility: you may rant and rave about how unfairly you've been treated and how much anger you are feeling. There are no rules about how you tell your story, and a hundred different scenarios may evolve. But, please release the steam valve—and soon.

Despite what we may have been taught, "taking responsibility" for our action or lack thereof does not mean *taking the blame*. Adding the secondary emotion of guilt to a heavily burdened conscience serves no purpose. Acknowledge, make amends if appropriate, and move on. Writing in a journal paves the way to a more restorative course of action.

The Ghostwriter

Despite my best efforts at writing personal diatribes, I've found that sometimes the issue is just too foggy, the feelings too fresh, the emotions too high to take the form of simple words and sentences. So I become the ghostwriter.

I write about my experience in the third person, telling "her" story instead of my own. I see myself through a frame of love and forgiveness, looking at my own missteps as I would those of a friend or sister faced with the same situation. As

"Writing provides the thinker with an opportunity to make visual contact with the contents of his mind."

—John Merriman

It was her first day on the job. She was so excited to be a new addition to the corporate world. She felt like a grown-up, but she wasnt. She was scared and shy and didnt know how to act or what to say. But she tried her best. She looked the part. She wanted so badly to impress, to be accepted, to be promoted in their world. And the male authority figures began to notice her. But not for the reasons she had hoped for. And when she saw how they reacted to her, she began to learn the way the system worked. They liked to look at her body more than they liked to hear her opinions. They noticed her legs and not her job performance. And gradually, she played right into their hands, abandoning herself and her dreams, and becoming the woman the office girls talked about in the break room.

illustrated in the story of the young and impressionable intern on the previous page, I have described a kind soul with a big heart who never intended things to end up the way they did. A child who is sorry for her actions. A girl who tried her best and failed because she simply lacked the level of understanding she now possesses—a most forgivable circumstance.

Taking on the role of the ghostwriter enables us to separate ourselves from a powerful event or overwhelming feeling, so that we can see it more clearly and without self-pity, anxiety, or spite. We can view our own actions as we would those of others, making us less judgmental, more understanding, and better able to heal our own wounds.

"Having my thoughts on paper where they wouldn't disappear helped me feel more in control."

—S. Walton

Sleepless

What to do about the more pervasive pressures underlying our daily existence—life without the circumstantial drama mentioned above? As much as I'd like to avoid cliché, there really is no other word that conjures up the image of that terrible tension expressed in the word STRESS. (It hisses even as you say it.) The hormonal changes created when the body experiences the stress-induced "fight-or-flight" reaction affect everything from appetite to aging. Stress is believed to cause disease and wreak havoc with metabolism. And perhaps

"It would be curious to discover who it is to whom one writes in a diary. Possibly to some mysterious personification of one's own personality."

—Beatrice Webb

the most common result of stress is loss of sleep. We are a country plagued by insomnia.

In reaction to this cruel nocturnal fate, some take pills; others drink herbal tea. Some read until the wee hours; some dive into a hot bath. **STILL OTHERS WRITE.** A number of options are available to those who choose the latter, and journaling, as described above, is one of them.

If taking the requisite time to journal will only serve to *increase* your stress level, here are some alternatives that require less time.

- *The Bitch Book*
  Healthy complaining can be safely spiral bound in a notebook for your eyes only. Getting your emotions out on paper is a private and respectable endeavor that may prevent unwittingly hurting others. So complain. Bitch. Kvetch. Express to de-stress.

- *B'Bye Box*
  Write a word or two on a napkin, a Post-it, a receipt— and place it inside this box. One rule: once you close the lid, you are not allowed to think about that particular subject—ever again. A quick way of letting go.

- *Bedside Burden Basket*
  It's nothing short of amazing how many thoughts and ideas occur to us the very minute our head hits the pillow. Often this leads to creative insight and more objective thought flow. It's wonderful! Unless, of course, we're trying to sleep. If something noteworthy crosses your bed-head, write it down and release it to the morning so you can get some shut-eye.

"To write is to transform that inward gaze into words, to study the worlds into which we pass when we retire into ourselves, and to do so with patience, obstinacy, and joy."

—Orhan Pamuk

"Sometimes I wonder if men and women really suit each other. Perhaps they should live next door and just visit now and then."

—Katharine Hepburn

Romance

We're all trying to figure it out—the formula, the science, the essence of being in love. We are drawn to it so magnetically that we will pursue its elusive call until death (or marriage) does us in.

For many, the unspoken language of physical attraction seems instinctual: we know what we like when we see it. It's the addition of communication that complicates the issue. Just ask Cyrano de Bergerac. When we consider the unification of the aptly named "opposite" sexes, relating to our loved one can seem downright impossible.

But trifling complications and insurmountable odds won't stop us mere mortals. Our hearts would seem bigger than our brains. We simply won't give up. And if that means buying a hundred self-help books, we will read until our eyes bleed simply to find "it." And if after fearlessly searching our whole lives for "it," we are among those lucky few who actually find "it," the question becomes, what do we do with "it"?

THE EVERYDAY LOVE NOTE

After generations of careful and courageous research on everything from love at first sight to the epidemic of infidelity to the effect of the football season on sex, most would agree that men and women think much differently. As a result, we fumble through romantic communications elicited from completely different sides of our lovers' wee brains. We shouldn't be surprised that we are often left scratching our heads. And doubtless there is a study on exactly which side of the head either sex chooses to scratch.

As much as we hate to admit it, the key to a better understanding of the opposite sex lies in a more, shall we say, literate form of communication than sex itself. So let's consider the ironically plausible, the ever-available, and the timelessly traditional option of words.

As you've surely noticed, words are wonderfully tricky. Such miniature strings of simple letters have the power to simultaneously provide both the solution and the problem. At times we feel abandoned by words, when even Mr. Webster can't properly describe what we're feeling. Often, despite our best intentions, we end up either stonily silent or inexorably verbose. We may say things we don't mean. We hurt more than we help. We end a potential relationship over the argument itself without addressing the underlying issue. It's enough to make a person head to the convent—until, of course, the concept of celibacy is considered. Best that we take a more cautious approach when composing our jumbled thoughts. After all, romance is a complex game.

Putting our sentiments in writing enables us to spend the necessary time to ensure careful and considerate communication with considerably less risk of misunderstanding. Better yet, letters are instantly intimate. Sealed with the tongue, letters whisper of secrets just between you and me. They elicit the childlike companionship of quiet conversation whispered among the crickets as the flashlight penetrates the glowing sheets of a sleeping bag fort.

Few gestures pluck at the human heartstrings quite like the old-fashioned love note. Infinitely warmer than e-mail, even more personal than a phone call, the handwritten note conveys far more than the sentiment written on the paper. It expresses the notion that the writer wants to spend some time with you, in thought, for just a little while.

The handwritten note says:
    I choose you
    I am speaking to you
    I value you

"More than kisses, letters mingle souls; for thus friends absent speak."

—John Donne

PASSION

I could use a little more passion in my life. How about you? Whether it's passion for an activity, a calling, or another person, rapture makes us feel alive. Seekers of this elusive electric charge might spend a lifetime in search of the one

> *"Be still when you have nothing to say;*
> *When true passion moves you, say what*
> *you've got to say, and say it hot."*

—D. H. Lawrence

thing that lights that inner fire, inspires forward movement, and makes us better people simply by aspiring to it. Other times the very object of our passion is right in front of us, yet we don't recognize its life-sustaining presence until it is gone.

When we are passionate about an endeavor, it is wholly receptive to our energies. The projects that readily absorb us are malleable channels for as much or as little as we want to give. On the other hand, passion for another person requires a much more specialized aim. Showing respect along with our admiration demands that we must constantly consider the person on the receiving end, carefully measuring his or her receptivity and personal threshold for thrill.

If you are among those lucky few who have found true passion for another person, actually recognize it for the vital necessity it is, and then receive equal passion in return, you will undoubtedly go to great lengths to capture it, to hold on tightly to its presence, and to ensure that it is always close by for sustenance.

But sadly, over time the lover's heart realizes that this possession, in itself, is impossible. Unlike a butterfly's wings forever pinned to black velveteen, you cannot hold the flame of passion any more than you can contain fire within your hands. It simply won't be captured. If the object of your obsession is alive, it *moves*. Human beings are human doings. And they are wont to move about in the most unpredictable ways. They are spontaneous and quirky, and will often go blindly where their immediate desires are first met. In addition to the capricious human nature, consider the constant demands of livelihood, a social sphere, and the intrigue of this vast and exciting world, and you might discover that sitting still long enough to be caught is virtually impossible. Those you love are compelled to go about their daily round on a distinctive course all their own, without you. And they undoubtedly will.

Modern man travels through time and space at a rate previously unmatched in history. So the question in this modern age of separated lovers becomes, how do two people keep from growing apart despite absence, independence, and the chaos in which we live?

Fortunately, the multiple modes of convenient communication available today ensure that we have no worthy excuse for falling out of touch. Putting our thoughts and feelings on paper is one of the most intimate ways we can reach out and touch the ones we love, whether they are across the breakfast table or across the continent.

Let's explore some of the ways in which today's busy person, who enjoys access to all possible forms of communication, can kindle the fires of true passion through writing.

"Epistolary intercourse."

—Letters, as defined by
Samuel Johnson

- *The letter*
  Inherently intimate, letters are *the* timeless classic of romantic overtures. Writing a letter requires the most intangible of human liberties—time. Any recipient worthy of time spent is unequivocally moved by an instant awareness of his or her value. In olden days, letters between estranged lovers were not a perquisite but a necessity—an essential method of circulating general news and of remaining "in touch." Two people separated by manifest destiny, the tragedy of war, or the hardships of primitive locomotion could not keep current on the events of the day or sustain communication without a postal connection. Consider, therefore, the enhanced value of the letter in the new millennium. Receiving a letter in this day and age has taken on an unusual cachet. It is a more unexpected surprise, a more graceful gesture than ever before. Imagine the carefully crafted loops and whirls, delivered in ink by one's own hand, scrolling across a sheet of fine paper and into another human heart—what a uniquely artistic concept! And when discovered amidst endless bills and solicitations, a personal letter or invitation becomes a rare delight more appreciated in today's fast-paced world. We no longer write out of duty but as a genteel expression of old-fashioned grace. Writing seems no longer an obligatory method of exchanging news but a conscious effort of purposeful deportment instead, instantly conveying a sense of closeness without physical presence.

- *Instant gratification*
  Speedy satisfaction has become our custom. Rarely do we have to wait or even leave the house for anything.

"Patience is a virtue" has been replaced by "Patience is powerlessness."

But even in this age of instant messaging, overnight mail, blackberries, and real-time computer cameras, human beings have still not mastered the technology of Mr. Spock's teleportation. The human touch remains a tactile sensation to be received in the flesh. And for the lover suffering from the chafing intolerance of separation, the waiting for a response from the beloved can breed an uncomfortable restlessness during which we begin to question the whole affair. Longing turns to intense frustration when we question the worth of a love that is incapable of any lasting endurance.

Fortunately for those who remain committed to relationships in face of this obstacle, this desire can be turned into an advantage, an opportunity to enhance rather than deplete. Spanning the distance of separation in a very tactile way, a well-written love letter conveys a longing that is palpable, sparking sensual imagination without constant need of physical sensation. Well-chosen words have the ability to touch, to flirt, to caress, and to soothe. The result? Desire is intensified, emotion magnified.

* *Proximity*

The trick to writing a romantic letter is to discover the secret to re-creating the closeness we crave. We can do this in a number of ways with pen and paper. First, we can be descriptive. The addition of those seemingly mundane details of daily life bring the recipient home to you. To remain close, one must keep abreast of "current affairs." We can also reminisce. Re-creating "old times" fosters a feeling of togetherness in memories shared between "just the two of us." Finally, use humor. Private jokes are a must that play especially well in the postscript. Imagine the recipient holding your letter, amused with a mild smirk or caught up in a wave of laughter.

"The weather is here. I wish you were beautiful."

—Jimmy Buffett

QUICK TIPS FOR THE QUICK FIX

In this age of often oxymoronic "modern romance," both men and women struggle with the arduous process of adjusting to our newly established roles as "equals." Unfortunately or fortunately, depending upon how you look at it, we are finding that the rules of courtship that guided our parents are either painfully cliché or simply inadequate in the face of modern relationships. Negotiating the distance between fierce independence and a deep need for companionship, we are often caught up in a clumsy dance, preoccupied solely with exactly *who* is leading.

And in my opinion, if this coveted position is truly up for grabs, I believe that it is *everyone's* responsibility to take the lead.

If you are in a relationship—male or female, just met or longtime lovers—reach out to someone in writing using these more modern modalities.

"Fill your paper with the breathings of your heart."

—William Wordsworth

• *Back to basics*

If you're not sure where to start, look back on how you got yourself into this male-female mess in the first place. Perhaps you were in fourth or fifth grade when you noticed him. And slowly, over time, you began to observe him more closely. And once you got past the somewhat distastefully foreign nature of a species so very different than your own, you yearned to learn more. One day, you received a carefully folded note passed surreptitiously across a chain of desks. And among the giggles, you read the following:

Will you go with me? Circle Yes or No

Your stomach did a little backflip—or was that your heart? (You never did learn to discern the difference.) *"Go where?"* you thought, as you picked up your pencil and gnawed anxiously at the eraser, glancing over his way. Would you dare to write back? The dance had begun.

And yet here you sit, fifteen or twenty years later, pen still poised above paper. *What is it that you wanted to say?* Coax those simple feelings to the surface, and write them down without censorship or judgment. Being unafraid to commit your unabashed feelings to paper is the essence of the love note.

• *Be childlike*

Place yourself gently back into the mind of the curious child you once were. Ask yourself what attracted you to this person in the first place. What did you initially notice? What first caught your eye? Reminisce about your initial interest in getting to know your companion.

> You always seemed apart from the others, like you had this special secret I couldn't help wanting to know.

• *Express gratitude*

What do you appreciate about this person? There is always something to be thankful for. It could be something simple: "I can always count on you to pull me out of my pity party." Or something more profound, spawned by a particular life event: "Thank you for involving yourself with my family after Dad died."

• *Be direct*

It is a bold endeavor to define your love for someone in concrete terms. After time you begin to know exactly what it is you are feeling. Take the next step and put it into words more specialized than "love" and "care." Be specific. Give examples.

> I don't know what I would do without your laughter around the house. It is the light that makes the windows glow, letting everyone know that we are home, that there is *life* within.

• *Compliment*
State your admiration. What do you like or respect about this person? What qualities would you like to emulate?

> I was truly amazed by the strength you possessed when you were cornered at the cocktail party last night. I wish I could be so poised in the face of such a confrontation. I am so proud of you. Will you teach me some of your social graces?

• *State the obvious*
No sentiment is too small, no thought too insignificant. We all need to hear loving observations as often as possible. Kind comments can deepen the intimacy in any relationship if we are willing simply to try. To avoid sounding trite, casually write what you would actually say aloud and in person.

> You are so nice to be around. Let me know when the next "Bring your husband to work" day is.

• *Start small*
If you're intimidated, take a look at the average-size gift card included with a bouquet of fresh flowers. Your words need not be sophisticated or elegant; your sentiment need not be lengthy. A simple "Thinking of You" will suffice. Written in your own hand, it is a gesture that is remembered long after the twentieth instant message is relegated to the cyberspace trash can.

> You have been on my mind all day. Hurry home!

- *Be vulnerable*
  Opening yourself to another person builds intimacy when it is done safely with a trusted soul. Such vulnerability requires honesty. Dare to say how you really feel.

  I wasn't sure how this weekend would go. I was really nervous. But being with you made the anxiety go away. It is so easy to like you.

- *Be clever*
  A Post-it note on the windshield reads, "Buckle up and bring yourself safely home to me."
  A cocktail napkin from your favorite restaurant reads, "See you at our table. 7 o'clock."
  A bookmark placed between the pages of a novel teases, "You read my mind. Love, Your Open Book."
  Place handwritten notes under the pillow, in a dopp kit or suitcase, the underwear drawer, or the jewelry box. Place a paper surprise in the medicine cabinet, the refrigerator, or the glove compartment.
  A briefcase yawns open on a Monday morning after a long weekend of social obligations and yard work. Your note waits patiently in his calendar and reads simply, "Thank you for giving me the gift of your time. Name ten ways I can repay you . . ."

"In a man's letters his soul lies naked."

—Samuel Johnson

"I want to cover every inch of you like ink on paper."

—Shawn Colvin

* *Be spontaneous*

    Don't wait for Valentine's Day. If a sentiment occurs to you, write it down and give it away. The unexpected love note is a cherished gift on a formerly mundane Thursday.

    So last night on the phone I was telling my sister about your penchant for finding just the precise word for everything. She said of your brilliant vocabulary, "Sounds like he's everything you ever wanted and desperately needed." Oh, by the way, she challenges you to a game of Scrabble sometime.

* *Be real*

    If you want to be loved for who you really are, take a risk by stating your truth. True intimacy enables us to be nakedly honest at the necessary moment.

    You are so cute in the morning. I adore your messy hair, those dreamy eyes, and your sleepy shuffle as you make your way down the hallway for coffee. I especially like it when you stop on the way to brush your teeth.

* *Avoid schmaltz*

    Like a good kiss, a good love letter avoids unnecessary drool. If we wanted love sonnets, we'd read Elizabeth

Barrett Browning. If we craved lust, we'd pick up a copy of *Cosmo*.

> Your nose is so darn cute. I just want to bite it off like a gumdrop.

* *Ask a question*
If familiarity breeds contempt, curiosity kindles flames. When you are in love with someone, you never reach the end of their being. Getting to know another person is an exciting lifelong quest that is thankfully never done.

> Lately I've been wondering what you must have been like as a child. How did you become the lovely person you are today? Tell me everything.

* *Use "I" instead of the universal "you" or "one"*
How easy it is to slip into figurative language when talking about our feelings. The quickest way to distance your paramour is to refer to some nebulous concept of a Romeo or Juliet you never knew. Two examples to avoid:

On marriage:
> When you find the right person in life, you just know it. Suddenly it's all you think about. You just want to spend all of your time with her.

Possible response:
> Who is SHE? Are you talking to ME?

You don't know a woman until you've had a letter from her.

On children:
> Having a child is a way to leave one's mark on the world, a piece of you that will be here after you're gone.

Possible response:
> Just *who* is 'one' planning on having this progeny with?

* *Determine your approach*

Whether loud or soft, subtle or bold, speak from *your* heart. Not someone else's.

> I've known you were the one for me since we met. I can't think of anyone I'd rather spend all of my time with than you. Let's make a life together.

* *Be a man*

One of the most tantalizing and romantic gestures a man can make involves writing out his feelings to a woman. Yes, that means you. The men we adore don't take timely expressions of affection for granted. They make it a point to remind us of our value again and again—and yet again. Remember: risk and repeat. Risk and repeat. This goes for women too!

I only have two tickets to the game. Please say you'll
come with me. I prefer you over the boys anytime.
You don't belch in my face.

Whether long and lovely or short and sweet, writing
meaningful love notes is incredibly easy in order to achieve a
positive impact on our relationships. Reaching out to those we
love with pen and paper is a small but significant step toward a
better understanding and a deeper intimacy. And it starts with
the simple and uncomplicated declaration of the affection that
brought us together in the first place—amid the heart flutter
of that first "love note." Surely you remember . . .

DEAR JOHN

For every relationship that thrives, another must end. Dating,
more often than not, involves breaking up. And in romantic
relationships when emotions are high, it matters not whether
you are the decisive closer or the jilted lover. Ending a
relationship with dignity, respect, and kindness is not a
simple task.

In my experience, there is nothing more crippling to
both parties than a cowardly prolongation of the inevitable
breakup. As we learn to trust our intuition—balancing realistic
expectations with consummate deal breakers—we gradually
build integrity when we have the strength to speak our truth
and to then act upon our beliefs. In relationships, this can
often necessitate a temporary separation, other times a step
back into friendship, and still other times the impenetrable
distance brought on by a succinct and final *adieu*.

Dear Romeo,

I'm afraid this has all gotten far too complicated. It started out innocently enough, but I'm afraid no one seems to agree that we make a good match. What with my family saying this and your family saying that . . . and all this late-night visiting has compromised my beauty sleep. How am I to attract a more socially appropriate suitor if I don't look my best? Not to mention the fact that I really can't see ending my life so soon. I'm only sixteen! I have my whole life ahead of me . . . and I do hope it includes a boy I can bring through the front door. Oh, Romeo! It was fun while it lasted, but I'm afraid this is "Ciao."
                                                    —Juliet

If you intend to show proper respect for another person (during a breakup or at anytime), it is always best to bravely deliver your truth *in person*. But before you go blindly into a potentially volatile situation, consider prudently putting pen to paper first. Putting your impression, your story, your experience on paper may help you to understand what has transpired and to begin the essential process of letting it go. In order to prepare to articulate the necessary message, take a few notes using the guidelines below.

GUIDELINES TO SPEAKING YOUR PIECE AND TO ACHIEVING YOUR PEACE

* *Be reasonable*
  Take note of some of the reasons that you wish to extricate yourself from this relationship. If you are still wavering in this decision, make a pro and con list. As clinical and cold as that may sound, list-making brings out our rational mind, a necessary tool in the face of important decisions. We can be more objective, less emotional.

  We have different priorities in life: home, stability, routine, future, safety, and planning versus risk, chance, adventure, travel, and chaos.

* *Be personal*
  Avoid "you" statements, which could imply blame. Instead focus on using "I" statements that refer to what *you* feel. This is especially important when listing specific examples that could lead to opposing positions of attacker and defender. Using "I" statements takes the

accusatory tone out of your comments and eliminates the need for the other person to become defensive.

> I have tried many different solutions in order to try
> and make this relationship work. I feel exhausted
> by the effort. I believe that if I continue to do this,
> I will lose myself in the process.

• *Be specific*
Cite the particular needs you have that are not currently being met in the relationship. Speak of your personal experience. Again, focus on "I" statements that do not emphasize the other person's failure to meet these needs.

> In order to be fulfilled, I need someone who is
> more focused on cultivating a spiritual life, someone
> who will be by my side as I discover God's place
> in my life.

• *Be objective*
If you wish to remain somewhat objective in order to clarify a point, refer to a specific *behavior* that you are unwilling to endure. Try the following formula:

> When you do X (specific action or behavior),
> I feel Y.

Example:
> When you give me unsolicited advice, I feel that
> you don't trust me, that you think I am incapable
> of making my own decisions.

NOTE: Action "X" referred to above must cite a specific *behavior*, not a general *attitude*. Avoid exaggeration and insult.

* *Be responsible*
Acknowledge the part you played in these circumstances. Take responsibility for your actions and make amends, if necessary. This may be your last chance to give and receive forgiveness, if forgiveness is to be had.

> I realize I haven't been as available to you as I should have, that I tended to be distant. I regret that I chose my job commitments over my family.

* *Be direct*
State your truth and let it be. No matter how painful it is to say good-bye or certainly to hear it, this person deserves to know the truth in order for both parties to move on. Prepare yourself for the consequences this may have.

> My intention is not to hurt you when I say that I just don't see a future between us. It's time we move on. I won't be calling you again.

* *Be at peace*
Sketch out some thoughts you feel you *must say* in order for the conversation to be complete. Do not let your fear censor you, causing you to leave important details and nuances unsaid. This may leave both parties unhappy and unsatisfied. Ask yourself: What would I like this person

to understand? Realizing, of course, that this is one goal you may not achieve.

I need you to know that despite my mistakes, I did the best I could.

THE LETTER NEVER SENT

In the fallout of romantic ruin, no response is the best response. Silence often speaks much louder than a tangle of words, however well-composed the missive. Sometimes we need a vent for our anger and frustration without the complication of involving the person who is the source of our pain.

How do we do this? You guessed it—with a pen. The most brilliantly scathing letter I have ever written was one that was never sent.

As we write out our most hideous thoughts, we have the ability to transfer their weight from our head to the paper. In doing so, we may freely assign blame, point the finger, express hate—even cast spells.

By writing the letter never sent, we alleviate the pressure of being *right* and can simply be mad. Yes! We can be childish, hotheaded, cowardly, even *wrong*. In the very heat of the moment, we can project our wrath onto the target of our choice without assuming any consequences.

As we write, the pages at our fingertips seem to absorb our agony, burning away rage and frustration. The only result is a soothing exhaustion and relief at having spit the proverbial nails.

T,

Do not think for a moment that your letter is in any way dignified by my response. Nothing you could have said could begin to explain your inexcusable behavior. I will remember you only as an unfortunate blight on my life.

I take a great deal of comfort knowing that I can be proud of the person I was when I was with you. I was whole-heartedly committed and entirely good to you. My conscience is clear. It cannot be so for you.

I do not hate you. You are not worthy of it. I do not even regret you. Exposing you for what you are has saved me, for I cannot fathom a worse fate than actually uniting myself indefinitely to such a monster.

You are dead to me. I am writing this only as a reminder than I can and will carry this scare into a better and wiser future.

       —M

Perhaps best of all, writing soothes the terrible need to feel understood. It comforts the aching soul, the wounded ego that cries out to be heard. So let your inner child babble and splash in a ritual as cleansing as the before-bedtime bath.

"Always write angry letters to your enemies. Never mail them."

—James Fallows

"*Handwriting is the closest thing we have to conveying human emotions with bone, muscle, and thought.*"

—Michael Sull

Correspondence

Reaching out to soothe the wounded knee of a fallen child; winding fingers gently around a lover's elbow at the threshold; placing the cradle of an arm round a parent's shoulder while taking in the view—soft, sweet, and subtle, the healing human touch is an instinctual response to another's need, an outlet for personal longing, and a uniting force that communicates all manner of emotion.

Human beings hold the power to comfort and calm with a caress. To subdue a sting and to steady a nerve with a gentle pat. *To heal with our very hands.* Indeed, life is full of celebrations and tragedies that present us with opportunities to reach out and touch another human being, to show that we care, to support, and to encourage.

But in this world of constant clamor and commotion, those we care about are not always within our limited reach. Those who need comfort most are often far away and beyond our healing human hands. How do we pull them close?

"The one good thing about not seeing you is that I can write you letters."

—Svetlana Alliluyeva

Rather than feeling frustrated by the potentially crippling distance that often exists between people today, let us consider words as an extension of touch. From minor boo-boos to major catastrophes, hugs have the power to heal. So it is with the written note—created and proffered by the human hand.

Communication through the written word has decreased in frequency due to a technological metamorphosis that mainly includes the birth of e-mail and the Internet. But letter writing remains an indispensable medium of communication, for often the most vital messages of the human spirit can be conveyed in no other way.

Written correspondence provides a more unique opportunity than ever before, because the social isolation engendered by modern technology forcefully compels us to reach out on a more personal level. Practiced pen pals find writing to be a more intimate medium, one that is capable of grappling with the intense emotions often involved in complex human relationships. While we often find discourse with another especially difficult in the heat of the moment, letter writing provides us the requisite time to access our rational minds. In this way, we allow emotions to diffuse quietly in order to purposefully choose our words and anticipate their possible interpretations, rather than carelessly launching them into another person's space. In fact, in a world of flat-screen computers and instantaneous text messages, writing seems the only medium capable of saving us from the chilling loneliness of a dismally digital world or the potentially fatal misinterpretation caused by ill-chosen speech.

This chapter provides guidance on how to conscientiously employ the healing human touch in writing humanity's most meaningful messages: condolences, gratitude, and reconciliation.

"Handwriting is purely a human activity that includes the inflections of personality and voice on paper. It can't be done by machine. When we lose handwriting, we've lost a precious sense of communication."

—Michael Sull

QUALITIES OF HANDWRITTEN LETTERS

Human
Generated by the fallible human hand, small errors once written cannot easily be disguised through deletion. This is a good thing. Handwritten notes need not be "letter perfect," as this is what makes them real and personal. And perhaps the awareness of exposing our humanness will encourage the writer to choose his or her words with more careful precision.

Personal
Each of us has a unique script that conveys our individual personality and style. Instead of trying to write as if recording

your words in a grade-school primer, consider your scribble to be a quirky part of your personality worth sharing with another human being.

Moving

Carefully crafted in flowing cursive or concisely cut in the angularity of block letters, mood is subtly but surely suggested to the reader in a way that no computer-generated font can. If we observe a person's script carefully, mysteries of character are revealed.

Tactile

The energy that is transmitted into the thinnest sheet of paper through human touch is locked in ink and can be felt across distance and time.

A Word on E-mail

Although there is indeed a place for electronic communication, letters of any sort of sentiment are certainly *not* an occasion for e-mail. Notes expressing condolence, gratitude, and reconciliation demand a hand! The qualities of a handwritten letter provide an essential human quality that lends deeper and essential meaning to our missives.

TIPS ON GETTING STARTED

None of us would ever *expressly* set out to write a letter like the one seen here—would we? Having just experienced firsthand how painful it is to read such pitiful drivel, we can almost laugh. Almost, that is, until the day we open

Dear Pen Pal,

Sorry I haven't written sooner. You know how I hate to write letters. I've been much too busy to take the time, but I feel obligated to write back because you insist on writing to ME. So I procrastinate as long as possible and when I finally force myself to sit down with pen and paper, I usually write something like this. . . . The first few phrases are usually spent apologizing for my pathetic lack of social decorum, often citing the number of exact days that have passed since last I wrote by saying something like, "I can't believe it's been X days since I received your letter!"

Then I go on to complain about how busy I am while trying to convince you that my lack of correspondence is NOT due to the fact that I don't care about you, or that I am a bad friend.

After I feel better for having made my excuses, I usually mention a few of my perpetual personal problems, just to make sure you're still paying attention. I refer to relationship heartaches, job struggles, and then add a few chronic health and financial issues that currently bog me down . . . and, of course, keep me from writing as often as I should.

I then apologize some more about what a lousy person I am, cleverly disguising this within compliments about how conscientious YOU are in your loyal efforts at communication.

And after a perfunctory salutation in assurance of my utter sincerity, I neatly sign my name, exhausted by the effort.

Basically, I try my very best to leave you wondering why on earth we are still friends after all these years when my letters aren't worth the price of a stamp.

Yours, Al Sohrann

the mailbox to find such a letter from an old high school buddy. Having been on the receiving end, we smugly assure ourselves that even on our worst days, we surely would *never* consider bothering our loved ones with such a pathetic excuse for a letter. After all, we safely avoid such blatant faux pas like blaming and complaining when socializing *in person*, but can we confidently say the same about our *written* correspondence? Or, due to our lack of practice and experience with letter writing, do we unwittingly repeat behavior so utterly lacking in tact on the rare occasion we begrudgingly unearth our favorite stationery?

If you are among those who would like to avoid such catastrophic communication, please read on.

Hello There!

Begin your letter with a warm and friendly salutation, just as you would upon greeting an old friend whom you haven't

In need of some inspiration? Sample the following book list.

84 Charing Cross Road, Helene Hanff
The Color Purple, Alice Walker
The Letters of Virginia Woolf, 6 vols.
Griffin and Sabine, Nick Bantock
The Screwtape Letters, C. S. Lewis
Letters to a Young Poet, Rainer Maria Rilke
The Habit of Being: Letters of Flannery O'Connor
Too Brief a Treat: The Letters of Truman Capote
Galileo's Daughter, Dava Sobel
The Diaries of Adam and Eve, Mark Twain

seen for a long time. Imagine yourself smiling as you begin your letter—if you'd like it to be read, that is.

> It's been too long since I've seen your face, so I'm writing to remind you of your dear friend who misses you.

Or

> Get ready for yet another fabulously exciting and much-anticipated letter from your cousin Emily. I have so much to tell you!

You would never greet a friend or family member with a slap in the face, so it's best to avoid abrupt negativity in your opening statement.

> I don't like writing. It takes too much time and I have nothing to say. I wish you'd step up to the times and get e-mail!

Or

> I am soooo sorry it's been soooo long since I've written. What with Jamie's exams and Martin with the flu, I've scarcely had time to take care of myself, much less . . .

The Pencil's Point
Yes, writing letters takes time. So does reading and responding to them. Be considerate of yourself *and* your audience by keeping your message simple and to the point. A basic letter has three parts: salutation, message, and closing. After supplying an inviting salute, decide on two or three things you'd like to say in the body of the letter. Ask yourself, "Why am I writing?"

Don't ramble on using the typical age-old fillers. Keeping to one or two pages will help the author remain disciplined and the reader remain interested.

Personality Makes It Personal

Be yourself. Use phrases and personal expressions that will help the reader recognize you in your writing. If it suits you, include lighthearted humor to convey your thoughts. If not, express your typical moodiness with darker, more sarcastic comedy. The goal is to let your individuality shine through, making the recipient feel as if you are in the very same room, sharing a personal conversation over coffee.

Sprinkle the letter with references, nicknames, or jokes only the recipient would understand. Doodle a small picture in the margin to illustrate an idea. Let quirky handwriting express your mood. Personal is the point. You want the reader to know that he or she holds a special place in your heart. Leave them with the feeling that they hope to see you again soon.

P.S. I think of you whenever I hear that song about piña coladas . . .

Reply in Kind

Make it clear to the recipient that you have "listened" well when reading his or her previous letters. Always refer to what was written to you *first*, answering particular questions and referring to specific life issues introduced in recent notes. Once these subjects are addressed, you can launch into personal news.

I was heartened to read that you felt the workshop was a success. Good for you! Let me know when you'll be hosting once again and I'll be sure to attend.

Keep It Casual

It is highly unlikely that the comments we make in our everyday social correspondence will be quoted on this evening's news, so why do we insist on contorting our thoughts in a game of mental Twister when we write letters? Often the inexperienced writer tends to assume an artificial and obviously affected formality when putting pen to paper. Ask yourself, is it your goal to communicate or to impress? I hope you find that when writing to friends and loved ones, it is unnecessary and insincere to bend and contort simple thoughts into lofty prose and stilted sentence structure. You don't have to don your Shakespearean tights and dramatically clutch your quill to write a meaningful letter. Simply *write as you would speak,* not as if you were reciting someone else's lines. You wouldn't want your letter to have to shout, *"It's me! Really . . . don't you remember me? It's your sister Katherine. It's me!"* If you put on false airs, the reader won't recognize or relate to you any more than if you were wearing a wig and dark glasses.

B'bye!

When saying your *au revoir,* don't stand on ceremony. Take leave in the letter just as you would depart from a friend's house after an informal get-together. As much as we might like to imagine that our few final words will leave the reader enriched and enlightened, gazing into the distance, awed by our keen insight, there is no need to attempt the profound here. It is not necessary to answer that nagging sociological question or to shed light on the essence of man in the closing of a letter any more than it is expected to delight everyone in the room with a witty one-liner just before you leave a party. Think of your closing as a casual wave rather than a dramatic *adieu*. You are not sobbing at an airport gate or riding off into a blazing sunset, duster flying. You are simply saying, "Until we meet again . . ."

Don't Delay!

If you pick up a sheet of your favorite stationery immediately after being regaled by a well-written letter, you will be much more likely respond in kind. Your prompt response will be fueled by fresh enthusiasm, having just encountered your good friend on paper. And perhaps best of all, you won't waste time apologizing for the delay in returning their affection, using excuses we have all heard countless times before.

"Don't use words too big for the subject. Don't say 'infinitely' when you mean 'very'; otherwise you'll have no word left when you want to talk about something really infinite."

—C. S. Lewis

Car-pool Cards
The most frequently used word in the English language would seem to be "time." Make the most of yours by creatively using moments in wait. A friend of mine keeps note cards, stamps, and pens in the door of her minivan and writes notes to friends while waiting in various parking lots for her requisite load of neighborhood children. Write, seal, and drop off into the nearest drive-through post office box.

No Whining!
In this world of constant activity, we often go long periods of time without seeing our family and friends. Although letter writing increases our sense of closeness, we cannot pretend to know exactly what someone is going through at any given moment. Therefore, it's best to use caution when sharing personal concerns. Avoid complaining of misfortunes that could be considered petty by those contending with greater problems. For example, it would be inappropriate to share the following with someone who has a terminally sick child:

> Junior is into absolutely everything and babbles a blue streak all day long. The house is in constant commotion from the minute he wakes up in the morning. He's just like his father—always into *something*. And he's growing so fast, I simply can't keep up with shopping for new clothes. Some days I just wish I had a little "me time," you know what I mean?

Dear friends,

Get ready for a little "holiday cheer" from the Foleys.

It's our traditional annual, much anticipated Christmas Letter!

We can hardly contain our joy that Joey, our eldest, just graduated first in his Harvard Law School class. And isn't he handsome! Just a chip off the old block! And if that weren't momentous enough, our baby girl Julia just won a scholarship to _Juilliard!_ And she's currently engaged to a _prince_ of a guy! (Literally! Won't it be difficult to choose between her violin and life in the family palace!)

We are so fortunate to be blessed with such a booming economy and have taken the opportunity to travel quite a bit this year. In expression of our gratitude for our momentous financial success, we have created a 3-D photo collage of our adventures this year. (Enclosed) Just look at Big Joe seated with Ambassador Chin on the Great Wall of China! We've had such a fabulous year, each success greater than the last. Wealth is ours and it sucks to be you! Ho ho ho!

Merry Christmas!

Show Off

We've all been victim to those incredibly overblown holiday letters that seem expressly designed to put the rest of us to shame. Produced by our more "successful" friends, these letters have one unfortunate result amidst the usual holiday cheer: to make the reader feel bad. The holiday letter is disguised as a friendly annual update intended to keep us abreast of the flourishing lives of our neighbors and relatives. These well-scripted and arrogant missives often endure for several pages, mentioning all the great success stories that point to their own good fortune. Painfully pretentious at best.

Happy Endings

Before relinquishing your missive into the capable hands of the U.S. Postal Service, ask yourself the following questions:

- Would I like to receive this letter?
- How would reading this letter make me feel?
- Is there anything in this letter that could be misconstrued or misunderstood by a particular reader?
- Would I allow a third reader to see this letter?
- Would I publish this letter in a newspaper with my name underneath it?
- Is this letter something I would like to be reminded of five years from now?

CONDOLENCES

When we encounter another person in pain, we feel compelled to put an immediate end to their suffering.

Whether due to our *own* discomfort in such situations or to our own desire to be heroic, seldom do we simply sit beside and allow others to live through and endure their own pain. For whatever reason, we feel called to come to the immediate rescue, providing just the right soothing verbal antidote to propel a person beyond their grief.

In our noble efforts to provide comfort, we are often frustrated by our own ineptitude at a task we have mistakenly attributed to personal responsibility. We simply don't feel up to the task of heroism on any given day. Unfortunately, our trepidation can lead us into an apprehensive silence that leaves the grieving person alone in sadness, or, alternately, can force us into clumsy efforts that potentially harm more than help.

At moments like this, we would do well to walk in the grieving person's shoes and question the rationality of these thoughts and feelings. For instance, would I, in my time of need, expect another person to whisk away my pain? Is there anything that anyone could offer that could alleviate my grief? Is it remotely possible that someone truly understands how much this hurts?

Sadly, the answer to these questions is often "no." The uncharted depth of another's personal suffering is a deep well not easily accessed by spectators.

Human beings cannot avoid the complex emotions associated with tragedy, nor can we simply remove them like a splinter from a wound. Given the limitations of our humanness, perhaps we are not called upon to summarily alleviate suffering. Perhaps we are merely asked to witness it, to provide presence and support to the best of our limited ability.

Dear S,

I got a call last night from Dad
telling me that his best friend has
passed on. Although impossible to
imagine the depth of your sadness,
I wanted you to know that our family
grieves beside you. When I think of
our old neighborhood, I first remember
the old brownstones, lined up like
soldiers guarding the slanted street.
Second, I think of your father. In my
childlike mind, he was one of those
brick soldiers-always there, watching
over us kids as we grew up playing on
the dirty sidewalks. I felt somehow
safe under his assumed care, despite
the wreckage that piled up around us
during those tumultuous times. I will
always love him for that.

I will be there Wednesday to hold your
hand and to celebrate the life of your
father.

Sincerely,

A

Accepting this truth reduces the anxiety we experience when writing a condolence letter. Relieved of the awesome responsibility of healer, we become a better "helper." The letter we write is no longer a panacea but simply a soothing reminder of presence. We are successful in our attempt at compassion when we provide a warm and comforting aspect that is content to quietly observe without judgment or proffered solution. Such is the essence of the condolence letter.

Writing a condolence letter is like holding a hand—a small action with the potential for enormous results. Here are some ideas that may help you in reaching out to a person in pain.

Disappointment Is Preconceived Expectation

Before beginning a condolence letter, it is best to adopt a selfless frame of mind. In this way, we become utterly aware of the recipient's personal boundaries so that we can make a subtle overture without inferring the slightest provocation. We should let go of any expectation that our words will somehow produce effect. Leave behind any thought of reciprocation in offering this "gift," and simply open your mind as you would your hand.

Stating Limits

In your condolence letter, state the one thing you can claim with certainty: "I am here." As suggested above, you are not expected to provide a cure, so don't try. The letter itself is a statement of your presence. Leave it at that.

> I know that there is little that I can say to help you through this tragedy. I am sorry that you are in pain. Please know that I am supporting you in spirit and sending you strength.

Practical Practice

Those who are experiencing personal tragedy often marvel in disbelief that the world can keep spinning with clockwork-like precision throughout the course of their grief. Mortgages demand to be paid, dogs howl to be walked, children cry out to be cared for, laundry has to be done. Not only is this often perceived as unfair to the grieving person but impossible as well. Sadness can be crippling, leaving those who suffer indifferent to their own needs. Although we cannot remove the anguish that causes this despondency, we can offer practical assistance to those who suffer in a small but significant attempt to lighten the life load of daily demands.

Avoid offering vague and empty promises such as, "Let us know if there is anything we can do" or "We are here to help—if you need us, just call." This puts the onus to act on those already burdened. Instead, make specific suggestions and begin preparing to execute them. There are a hundred tasks that can be offered that go far beyond the casserole dish. This may require a little research through family and friends closer to the mourning.

> I understand that your parents arrive on Tuesday afternoon. Allow me to pick them up at the airport. I will call you (and your parents) to confirm.

Or

> I would like to pick up your children Saturday morning at 10 a.m. and take them on a family outing. I will confirm with your husband.

Hope's Well Springs Eternal

In their inability to see beyond the immediate pain, those who are facing difficult times often feel a tremendous hopelessness. If you have experienced a similar difficulty (never assume it is identical), perhaps others could benefit from your strength and experience. This honest sharing of one's self often plants a seed of hope in the sufferer's heart. In this instance, we do not belabor our own troubles. Rather, we tell a personal story that reflects the positive aspect of overcoming our own misfortune.

> I'm not sure if I ever told you this, but I was fired from my "dream job" a few years ago. It was an incredibly difficult time. I think the hardest part was the blow it dealt to my sense of self-worth, knowing that others had judged me to be inadequate. It hurt. At first, I panicked and began a desperate search for work. But I found I was unable. All I could do at the time was accept my devastation and strive to remain upright, however immobile, trying not to let depression claim me as the dust began to settle. And as I allowed myself time and rest, I began to gain perspective. (Of course, this entailed many an exaggerated and bitter retelling of my painful firing to friends and family.) Slowly I emerged from the wreckage—wiser about my true calling and a little tougher as well. I wish you the strength I found with time.

Feelings . . . Nothing More Than Feelings

Sometimes in the bravado spawned at the recollection of having surmounted personal obstacles, we slip into the inference that we know another person's mind. To assume another's feelings is to belittle another's pain. None of us can pretend to claim total understanding of another's suffering, so let's not try. Avoid such statements as "I know exactly how you feel. When I went through my divorce, I thought the world would end" or "I understand just what you're going through. I've never actually experienced chemotherapy, but I can imagine what it's like as I don't deal well with nausea."

Death by Cliché

When a person is in the throes of anguish, it is not beneficial to suggest that a simple attitude adjustment would alleviate their suffering. This type of advice is only made worse by offering painful clichés about the bright side and the cup half full. While it may be perceived as helpful to the person delivering this vapid commentary, trite statements can trivialize grave situations by offering simple solutions to difficult problems.

As I always say at times like these, "This too shall pass."

Just be patient.

Time heals all wounds.

The Vice of Advice

Because we cannot truly understand another's grief, we cannot offer ready solutions to others' problems. Even if we are close to the fire in a particular disaster, we must accept that each person reacts much differently to the heat. We cannot solve an issue that is not our own.

If I were you, I'd get right back on my horse and ride.

Don't forget that you have two other children to care for. Maybe busying yourself being a mother to them would help you forget about Tim's illness.

You can always buy another dog.

Thy Will Be Done

If we are respectful of where we end and where another person begins, we will avoid making references to a greater force at work or drawing conclusions about the possible purpose behind a seemingly random act. Even if our own experience is drawn upon faith or a particular mode of reasoning, we should avoid proselytizing. We may do more damage than we realize if we insist upon speaking of Fate, God's will, or the complex workings of a chaotic universe.

We must accept in these sorrowful times that this loss was somehow intended, that it was meant to be part of a greater plan. The sooner we accept that a power beyond our understanding is at work, the sooner we can get on with the business of life.

Think of the condolence letter as a warm handclasp. Provide presence without judgment, assistance without solutions, and experience without advice. These skills can be tricky, but if we place ourselves in the position of recipient, we need only consider what we might like to hear in our own time of need.

GRATITUDE

First off, let's get one thing straight: *Everyone* owes *someone* a thank-you. Gifts, of course, are a given. Presents of any kind must be answered in some form of written gratitude that goes beyond a simple "confirm receipt." But there are many other nonmaterial gifts we receive every day that risk going unappreciated or, as the giver may perceive, totally unnoticed: small acts of favor, selfless tasks, gestures of goodwill, kind deeds. It would be a sad world indeed if we didn't express grateful acknowledgement of human perceptiveness, sincere empathy, shared laughter, and spiritual support.

In the professional realm, thank-you notes are simple common sense. Post-interview appreciation, gratitude for advice or assistance, acknowledgement to those behind the scenes, celebration of a sale—testimonials that build camaraderie and foster teamwork will be remembered long after the favor is proffered.

Whether it is of a personal, professional, familial, or romantic nature, relationships are enhanced by small acknowledgments of presence. And let's not forget those brief chance encounters that mysteriously and permanently alter our life's course. All involved would benefit from honoring the all-essential contribution of the fleeting acquaintance.

Unfortunately, unless it's delivered tongue in cheek, we seldom have the opportunity to write fill-in-the-blank thank-you notes. And there are times when, out of sheer obligation to social etiquette, we are called to send a note of appreciation for an item or action we might not truly have appreciated—but isn't it the thought, or the seeming lack thereof, that counts?

"In the faces of men and women I see God, and in my own face in the glass, I find letters from God dropped in the street, and every one is signed by God's name. And I leave them where they are, for I know that whereso'er I go, others will punctually come for ever and ever."

—Walt Whitman

If you pick up the average thank-you note, you will see that often our expressions of gratitude are so generic that they could be written to anyone about anything. Following are some tips to make a somewhat necessary social task into a more precise and pleasing personal pleasure.

Quick Draw McGraw

The best thank-you notes are written in the immediate wake of a gift or gesture received. When the ribbons are freshly cut and the gift is noisily unearthed from a bed of crackling tissue paper, when the lightbulb flashes brilliantly above in sudden realization of a favor done, when the ink on the dotted line is still wet—it is at these moments that a flood of emotion is all the fuel we need to sit down with pen and paper. If we are prompt in our responses, those to whom we owe gratitude will feel the genuine appreciation that drove us excitedly to the post office when gratitude suddenly became our foremost priority.

Dear Auntie Holiday,

Thank you so much for the lovely _____.
(NAME GIFT HERE)

It was so _____ of you to think of me while on
one of your famous shopping sprees.
(DESCRIPTIVE ADJECTIVE HERE)

You couldn't possibly have known _____.
(CHECK ALL THAT APPLY OR ADD YOUR OWN)
___I'm allergic.
___We already have four others.
___Ed moved out six months ago.
___I pawned my television.

You seem to have selected one item I would never have
purchased for myself because _____.
(CHECK ALL THAT APPLY OR ADD YOUR OWN)
___We're financially strapped.
___I lack the necessary taste.
___This item serves no purpose.
___We actually don't have a dog.

This _____ will always remind me of your _____.
(CIRCLE TWO)
Kindness   Compulsive spending   Ineptitude
          Generosity   Cluelessness

Again, sincerest thanks for assuming I'm just tacky
enough to re-gift!

Gratefully,

Kat

FIRST CLASS

Sotheby,

You won't believe what just happened. The buyers agreed to our price as it was originally listed! I feel relieved and exhilarated all at the same time. I can't wait to tell Jim! But first, I wanted to sit down immediately to write you a note of sincerest thanks. We could not have done this without your expert advice, constant support, and unique ideas. You'll be invited to our new house for a champagne celebration!

Until then, Rich

It's Not Easy Being Perfect

Choosing a truly appropriate gift is a rare talent much more complicated than mere super shopping. Knowing the right words of advice and how to deliver them without preaching is a gift enjoyed by the truly perceptive. Choosing the appropriate medium for showing support without belittling the ego requires true insight. How do we show that we are cognizant of another's effort, skill, or divine inspiration? We praise the giver's insight into our person, our character, and our specific need.

Dr. Spock,

Have you been spying on us? You must have been. I can't fathom how else you might have known that we are struggling (read: pulling our hair out) in the face of the terrible twos. You must somehow have known what we're going through. That in itself is a comfort. So, tell me, does it ever end?

I've heard of this book but haven't taken the time
to check it out between temper tantrums and potty
training. And when our son is president someday, I'll
have you to thank for it.

Sincerely, Mama Mia!

Useful Measures

The best way to articulate your appreciation of an item or
gesture is to specifically illustrate its particular benefits in
your life. The more personal the gain, the better. Ask yourself,
"How did this action or gift make my life better, easier, more
pleasant?" If we are specific, we again give credit to the giver's
sense of intuition and propriety.

Wisteria,

My back doesn't hurt anymore! Leave it to a green
thumb like you to know how the right pair of shears can
save a gardener's spine. More than a chiropractor, the
massages, the acupuncture, and the hot salt baths, this
is a gift that will keep on giving. Please know that the
spring glory of my hyacinths and daffodils will be due
to your kindness.

Regards, Ms. Mudd

Vague Isn't Vogue

In situations where the gift received is "intangible," we
may find ourselves tending toward inexplicit expressions of
gratitude. It is the rarest and most beautiful of gifts that pose

the greatest difficulty when articulating appreciation—those quiet gestures, expressions, and meaningful tokens of human kindness that make manifest the noblest purpose of our lives on earth: To make lots of money and buy expensive gifts? No! To serve others? Yes!

Vague:

Mr. So & So,

I truly appreciate your being there for me. I don't think I could have gotten through this weekend without you. Thank you for your support.

Yours, Bland

Vogue:

Angel,

What could I have done without your constant presence this weekend at Mom's funeral? I don't think I could have negotiated the perfunctory small talk if you hadn't been standing beside me, propping me up. Thank you for making sure I didn't retire with a sleeping pill to my room during the reception. The soup and red wine by the fire in comfortable silence was much more beneficial to my spirit. I appreciate your help with the dishes and leftovers. My freezer is always open to you, my true friend.

In sincerest gratitude,
Ambien

It's a Gusher!

Although we may be quite moved by another's kindness, it's best to keep thank-you notes simple and straightforward—validating the gesture and stating its blessings. Flowery language and hyperbole may actually demean the giver, being perceived as exaggerated and insincere. While it's fine to recognize another's sacrifice or intuition, we should not assume that they acted to their own detriment when they loaned us the weed eater. Such is the stuff of Shakespearean tragedy.

Hamlet,

I have never before been so touched. It is friends like you who make my life worth living. I will never forget your heroic kindness during this terrible flu season. Your chicken soup was divine!

Yours,
William S.

Quick Tips for the Right Quips

• *Gifts*
State the particular benefit you received by illustrating your enjoyment of it.

• *Favors*
No gesture is too small to go unnoticed; honor thoughtfulness in others.

• *Professional*
Recognize another's participation in helping you achieve your goals.

* *Occasions*
  Promptly express the joy experienced at a
  memorable event.

* *Intangibles*
  Name the specific item or action that incited
  your gratitude.

* *Beneficial bliss*
  Deep personal satisfaction comes from knowing
  that amidst the chaos of this modern world, you
  recognized an act of human kindness.

So if you have been fortunate enough to witness the greatest
capacity we humans possess—to do good—sit down with pen
and paper and give gratitude a try. And as you lick the seal,
apply the stamp, and pop your personal thank-you note into
the mailbox, take note of a barely perceptible lightness in your
step. You may also experience a sensation of warmth, a certain
weightlessness, or a sudden energy of spirit. Those who
cultivate a lifelong habit of writing thank-you notes begin
to reap benefits beyond their imagination. Not only does
acting on gratitude fill a tremendous social need, it also lights
the soul with a perception of purposefulness, an unearthly
connection, and a glowing sense of pride. What better way to
become a participant in the deed of giving?

It's quite simple: Writing thank-you notes makes the world
a better place—even if it's just for a brief and beautiful
moment in time, your tiny glimpse of paradise.

U.S. POSTAGE
00.29 3
H METER580491

*"But words are things, and a small drop of ink,
falling like dew, upon a thought, produces that
which makes thousands, perhaps millions, think."*

—Lord Byron

RECONCILIATION

**APOLOGY: AN ACKNOWLEDGMENT EXPRESSING REGRET FOR A
WRONG, IMPROPER, OR DISCOMMODING ACT**

"Discommoding?" I'll say! In fact, I find the personal trauma
surrounding apologies to be a damned inconvenience.
Apologizing interferes with my best-laid plans to be the first
perfect person to walk the earth. Do any of us ever relish
admitting when we're wrong? Personally, humble pie has
never been my favorite dish, and I can't say I like the taste of
crow any better. But after frequently encountering my own
words in a bowl of alphabet soup, I can say that I've become
better at apologizing over the years, because practice makes
perfect and I'm wrong a lot.

Open Mouth—Insert Foot
Making amends is a tricky endeavor. As the above expression
illustrates, first it involves sufficient flexibility. Second, it
involves admitting fault—and who wants to do that? And
third, although we'd like to be sure that our apology will
be accepted with diplomacy and understanding, we seldom
know this with any certainty in advance. Atonement involves

Dear Black Widow,

I am sorry that I resorted to such
petty and childish behavior the other
night upon discovering that you had
(once again) lied to me. I admit my
temper tends to flare when I am made a
cuckold by someone I love. Perhaps if
you were as true to me as I deserve,
you wouldn't incite my lowlier instincts. Enclosed, please find $50 to
contribute to his bloody nose fund.

Wronged

"Letters are largely written to get things out of your system."

—John Dos Passos

risk. We must face our fear of rejection, judgment, and even retaliation. But at the end of the day, no matter what the outcome, the hope is that we feel less burdened, leaving behind guilt, shame, regret, and other soul wreckers.

The boldest way to make amends to another person is in written form, where our words are permanent and alive, our thoughts more rational and composed, our temper safely harnessed. This takes preparation and practice. Let's get started—before our next boo-boo.

Price of Admission

Much like an actor in a specific role, we all play some part in the acts of our life drama. Whether it was misunderstanding, miscommunication, or simply missing the bus, accepting responsibility for the part you played is a first and essential step in the process of forgiveness.

As stated previously, acknowledging personal fault does *not* mean taking the blame! Your action (or lack thereof) may not be the shift that caused the avalanche, but honesty demands that we recognize our own contribution to the rubble. The sooner we fess up to our participation, the sooner our arms and hands become open enough to receive forgiveness with humility. So pay the price of admitting your mistake and get it over with. *Mea maxima culpa!*

First off, let me just say what a jerk I've been lately. As soon as I realized the ego trip I was on, I sat down to write you an apology. I immediately felt as if I'd done something *right*. I must be capable after all.

And Make It Quick!

Relationships can often turn into a dangerous battlefield riddled with confusion, pride, anger, and rebellion. When a volatile argument is then reflected on paper, an essential survival skill involves knowing when to retreat. Without the benefit of facial expression and tone of voice, one has no hint as to the reader's frame of mind. Our words must literally speak for themselves. So in delicate emotional situations, it's often best to simply state your part, express your regret, cease and desist. Cleanly and directly cite the misstep, admit you're sorry, and stop writing.

I am sincerely sorry for missing your recital, because I know how much it meant to you. My inexplicable shift in priorities does not properly reflect how much I care about you. I apologize. I'll be there next time.   Forgetful

Beggar Begone

As counterintuitive as it might sound, the apology letter is not the time or place to ask forgiveness. Humility suggests taking atonement one step at a time. This allows time for contemplation and healing, and a vent for the dissipation of angry steam. If you are writing to someone solely to receive immediate confirmation of your worth or status as a person (and not as a pool of miserable pond scum), perhaps you are not quite ready to express your regret. The very essence of

making amends involves stating your truth while remaining
willing to accept any consequence. Karma is a force beyond
our control. Ironically, when asking forgiveness, we need not
ask. We extend an open hand in the hope that someone will
take it.

Avoid:

> Believe me, I *know* we can get past this! Say you'll
> forgive me so we can move on. Besides, my cousin's
> wedding is next weekend and I need to know if I'll
> have a date!

Instant Replay

As much as you may be tempted, an apology letter is not
your personal opportunity to relive the entire episode on
paper. Before writing, ask yourself *why* you might feel the
urge to rehash the incident yet again. Is it to settle unfinished
business, assign blame, or make one last excuse for your
behavior? Consciously or not, by purposely reliving another's
pain, for example, you are indirectly stating that the person
you have offended wasn't paying attention the *first* time. This
is not a documentary or a testimonial or your own eulogy.
It's a note of apology. We cannot undo what is past. Save the
instant replay for your journal. Redress is not always the road
to reparation.

Avoid:

> And then when you said you didn't give a damn, it felt
> like a punch in the gut. At that point, I just wanted to
> leave. But I didn't. I stayed and kept trying to resolve
> things. Surely that's worth something!

"Well, excuuuuuuse me!"
Steve Martin made this phrase famously funny back in the seventies. But in times of true remorse, sarcasm is best left to the masters of comedy. People who are genuinely sorry for their mistakes do not rationalize their behavior. Justification of one's actions is a transparent attempt to deny responsibility. Rationalization is a shifty method of quietly assigning the blame. Whereas when we are truly willing to make amends, we let go of *all* our excuses, laying our regret at another's doorstep with dignity and self-respect.

Fortunately, relationships rarely play out in a court of law. Better to leave "mitigating circumstances" to the lawyers. Not to mention, pleading one's case is unflattering at best and reflects poorly on one's obviously desperate need for pardon. Remember the power of true humility; remain wary of your tendency to make excuses, which can seem to trivialize a serious situation, leaving another insulted at your apparent lack of feeling.

Avoid:
> Things would have turned out much differently if you hadn't stormed out on me like that. If you had just stayed home with me last night, this never would have happened. How could I have known she'd come over in such a state? If only I'd been sober. I'm sorry, sweetheart! But it wasn't **MY** fault.

Hand Washing
There is a certain freedom in being able to accept our mistakes and to acknowledge them on paper to another person. There is satisfaction, however grim initially, in finding

the necessary humility to admit our imperfections. If we are willing to admit our wrongs, we are open to growing beyond them. The apology letter is the gateway to forgiveness and serenity, no matter what the final outcome, if we are willing to swallow our pride and taste a little humble pie.

The Last Word

Congratulations! You've taken the necessary time and care to write your letter. You've placed a sheet of fine paper lovingly inside the waiting envelope and raised it to your lips to moisten the seal when suddenly it hits you, your hand stuck in midflight halfway to your chin: one all-essential key remark has been left out of your missive, and it's something you absolutely, positively must say.

For all those left unsatisfied by the limits of their letter-writing ability, the P.S. is for you.

The beauty of the postscript is that it affords us one more chance to express what we may not have stated in the body of our letter. In fact, the P.S. often contains the small but essential truth we've been thinking about all along but didn't know how to say. The P.S. is often the very essence of our letter. It's where we make our final point. It's the last word.

Whether a direct dictum, a spontaneous declaration, a clever comment, a basic truth, a poignant point, or a mysterious question, the P.S. commands the reader's attention.

Whether adding an explanation point or having failed to make your point, the P.S. gives you one more try. It's the short, sweet, cunning, clever, and very conscious addition at the end of a letter that becomes the anchor of all truth: the P.S. —how we love you.

Curtain falls . . .

p.s. Please say you miss me too.

P.S. I'm hooked!

p.s. Don't you think we could be happy?

P.S. This makes my year!

p.s. It's up to you now

P.S. I will never forget this day.

P.S. Join me?

P.S. I've never felt this way before.

P.S. Why not?

p.s. I'm waiting . . .

"A woman seldom writes her mind but in her post script."

—Richard Steele

Deer Gramaw,

When ~~Mommy~~ Mommy gets a gift she says OH! you shoodnt have but you can tel she doesnt meen it. I want you to no that I think you SHOOD HAVE and I'm shur glad you did! Thank you for the Tommy twysteroo. I will share it with you when you come next time to play.

I love you, Gramaw.
Tom

Family

It's a fact: Right now, at this very moment, mothers and fathers everywhere are losing sleep over their children. Haunted at night by words whispered during parent-teacher conferences—"peer pressure," "social adjustment," "behavioral issues," "noncompliance," and "ADD"—it's no wonder that parents across the globe are plagued by insomnia. Ironically, if ever there were a group of people deserving of proper rest, it would be modern-day parents. Not only do they have the extraordinary job of raising our future society, but they are also among the most *exhausted* people on earth. Why? Because they've seen it all—the terrible two-year-old, the egocentric kindergartner, the introverted grade-schooler, and the pimply faced, surly teen who communicates (albeit rarely) through a perpetually locked bedroom door. Parents who survive these various stages of childhood—mental faculties intact—can then look forward to encountering the depressed, poorly dressed, aloof college student, whose poetically pointless lifestyle they continue to fund.

Rearing our progeny from womb to classroom to board-room is not an easy task. But because we believe in the tremendous importance of our role as parents, we refuse to give up. We tirelessly strive to raise good people of whom we can be proud. If we are realistic, we look if not for perfect grades, then for *effort*. If not for outstanding artistic ability, then for *creativity*. And if not for a prodigy, then for a child who "plays well with others," which happens to be my personal favorite.

I happen to think that "plays well with others" is what it's all about. The highest of compliments, this classification drawn from the grade-school report card describes a moderate person who espouses all the social graces enjoyed by well-adjusted people: sharing, courtesy, kindness, gratitude, and, of course, conscientious communication.

If you are currently facing the awesomely critical task of child-rearing, and the ideal described in "plays well with others" is a standard you strive to engender in your offspring, this chapter will reveal a unique way in which you can send your child on a lifelong journey of appreciation, awareness, discipline, accountability, and the immense freedom found through self-expression.

GETTING STARTED

Parents know better than anyone that kids need the proper equipment to learn any new skill. Soccer season means shin guards and jerseys. Ballet brings pink tights and black leotards. And when September rolls around, it's a school box overflowing with shiny new supplies. If we hope to teach children how to connect mind to paper, we need to give them the "write stuff." Thankfully, no costly trip to the store is required! Most of these writing supplies are readily available in your very own desk drawer.

Let's look at the typical toolbox of the budding writer.

The Writing Kit

In order to foster a sense of play regarding written correspondence, it's a good idea to present these writing tools as toys. Surprise your child with his or her very own Writing Toolbox. You could unearth a simple shoebox and wrap it in decorative paper or use a Rubbermaid bin decorated with fun stickers, decals, and paint pens. Inside this little treasure trove, your child will find all the accoutrements he or she needs to make writing notes and letters an enjoyable lifelong habit.

Paper Chase

Ideally, we'd like our children to be enthusiastic about writing notes. Stationery for kids should be whimsical and fun. Allow your children of discerning age to choose their own stationery according to a favorite theme, concept, or color. If you want junior to consider writing as a project of his own, follow his unique personality and demeanor when choosing the perfect paper instead of inflicting your own more formal style upon him. In my opinion, forcing extra fancy notes on your wee daredevil, for example, is almost like squeezing him into last year's starched white Easter outfit. It just doesn't fit. If elegant letterpress or engraved stationery is a must-have, choose a light, bright, childlike color or theme in keeping with your little one's age.

In my stationery design business, I once had a four-year-old client who stated her own design preference emphatically with a single word: bugs. And bugs are just what she got! Many of the large "everything stores" are full of wonderful stationery for children that won't break the bank. Or perhaps you could spare a few of your own more playful note cards when creating your child's first writing kit.

Mine

Kids who are learning their letters like to see their name in print. It seems most adults never tire of it either. Personalized or monogrammed stationery is a way to give budding letter writers a sense of ownership and pride. We all know how much kids like to say "MINE!" So in this case, let them. The hope is that children will begin to make the process of correspondence their own: "My stationery means my responsibility to write thank-you notes."

Color

In a child's world, color is just a whole lot more fun than black and white. Every child's writing kit should have plenty of markers, crayons, colored pens, and pencils. Kids can mix it up, have fun, and be creative. One paragraph might be written in blue. Another in red. The signature might be a lettered rainbow. This is especially important for young children who are just learning to write, or who can't yet write at all. Drawing pictures is a wonderful way for a child to express his or her thoughts to another person, inevitably brightening everyone's day in the process.

"Words are your paint. Use all the colors."

—Ray Alexander

ABCs

As children get older, they can be taught to maintain their own roster of addresses. It's up to you to provide some kind of notebook for this purpose. Perhaps you've received a free calendar or address book from your local bank, and it's sitting quietly unused in your desk drawer. Maybe you could adapt a simple wire-bound steno pad into an address book by making alphabetical letter tabs out of Post-it notes.

Learning to stay socially connected by tracking the whereabouts of our contacts is a skill essential to everyone—whether businessperson, social butterfly, mother, or loyal friend. Anyone who's ever sent out a holiday card to a large list of friends, family, and colleagues knows the secret of saving the tiny but essential upper left corner of the envelopes they receive. Many adults today have conveniently relegated this information to the Palm Pilot, the Blackberry, or the administrative assistant, but a child has to start somewhere. In keeping an address book, children are introduced to the tenuous nature of human transience. Your child will become aware that in this enormous and intriguing world of places to go and people to meet, sometimes it can be an effort just to sit still—and not everyone does. Just because our friends have always lived right up the street doesn't mean they always will. Thankfully, no matter where our loved ones may roam, we can always keep in touch.

Stamp of Approval

Not all mail is electronic mail—a novel idea to a child of the next generation. Imagine explaining to your child the veritable magic carpet ride taken by a stamped envelope. The simple addition of a colorful little decal known as the postage stamp represents an adventure in communication, commerce in motion: "A postage stamp is sort of like gluing pennies from your piggy bank onto an envelope to pay its way—only the stamp travels much lighter. Let's stick it here in the upper right corner, like this, and walk it to the mailbox. Later on, unless it's a Sunday, the mailman will come to our house, pick it up, and take it to your friend Josh's house—all for forty-one cents!"

Far beyond the red, white, and blue of the classic American flag, there are always whimsical postage stamps available that are more fun for kids—and adults. At usps.com, you can conveniently purchase stamps by mail that feature nursery rhymes, children's books, significant authors, and celebrated talents—true heroes of literary, scientific, and cultural history. In 2005, Jim Henson and his Muppets were so honored. In 2006, we had Mickey Mouse, and Wilbur the Pig from *Charlotte's Web*. *Where the Wild Things Are* arrived in 2007.

Your child may encounter a controversial Kobe Bryant on the Wheaties box tomorrow morning, but he won't likely find Dr. Seuss—and it would be a pity not to know *him*.

Letter Box

To complete your child's Writing Toolbox, provide them a safe and secret place to store the letters and cards they receive. If there's no more room under the child's bed, and such treasures risk getting lost, I suggest that parents keep this

> *"A student can win twelve letters at a*
> *university without learning how to write one."*

—Robert Maynard Hutchins

collection of missives safe until the child is old enough to take proper care of it. Letters, like photographs, tell stories, and while they are certainly to be enjoyed in the moment, their value only increases with time.

Childhood is a critical period of formation during which we develop the habits and skills that will carry us into adulthood. It is a process that passes by, sometimes quickly, other times slowly, right before our very eyes. If we watch carefully, we'll witness ringleaders turn into world leaders, bullies become ballerinas, and tricksters turn into teachers.

No matter what their future calling, children who are taught the value of the written word will provide benefits beyond your imagining. The time to begin is now.

THE LUNCH BOX NOTE

In case you hadn't noticed already, it's a tough world out there, especially on the playground. Stories of schoolyard chaos and cruelty seem to become more prevalent and more heartbreaking every year. Although we wish that school were a completely secure place for the precious young souls who enter there, it is often where children first stumble upon some painful but necessary social stepping-stones after leaving the

Surprise!

I would have waited until after school today, but I had something very important to tell you that just couldn't wait.

I just wanted you to know that no matter what words appear on your spelling test today, or who gets chosen first at recess, your Mom and Dad love you and we can't wait for you to come home and tell us all about it tonight at dinner.

Love, Mom

"There must be millions of people all over the world who never get any love letters. I could be their leader."

—Charlie Brown

security of family and home. Because the social interaction encountered at school is the foundation for a child's first interpersonal vision of the world, sending children to school prepared for this important step means more than providing galoshes and a windbreaker for recess. Kids need to wear a strong armor of familial support just as a turtle sports his shell. And parents need to supply constant reminders of stability, security, and love that kids can carry from curbside carpool to classroom.

Remember the sense of wonder you felt upon discovering a small handwritten note wedged underneath your warm and melting peanut butter and jelly sandwich; the tiny thrill that made you look coyly over your shoulder, wanting to guard this private encounter as your very own; the flush that spread across your cheeks, half in embarrassment, half in a deep sense of joy and pride? If you have ever been among those lucky few to receive a lunch box letter, you know the power of a few carefully chosen words written by Mom or Dad.

The essence of the lunch box letter is to produce spontaneous emotion through the element of surprise, offering a gesture of unconditional love in its wake. The sentiment expressed to your child is that "no matter what happens *out there*, I'm *here* and I care." The idea that we can periodically provide such validation to our loved ones extends far beyond the lunch box.

Playground Protection

Choosing up teams, executing dares, getting jump rope welts and skinned knees—life on the blacktop can be brutal. Children running wild at recess are subjected to all sorts of real-world nasties—competition, ridicule, gossip, aggression, and, perhaps worst of all, that devastating social wrecking ball—the clique. Taken together it would seem a good case for home schooling. But the child who carries a lunch box letter—that special reminder of a parent's affection and support—might not take it to heart when the class bully pronounces him a loser, or he's chosen last for kickball, or another round of nicknames is doled out. The lunch box letter is a sort of protective talisman to remind a child of his or her inherent goodness.

Do What I Do

When you send your child a letter, whether delivered via the lunch box or the toy box, you lead by example, showing the child that you practice what you preach. Children also learn that it is good to share a bit of ourselves with those we love, that there is value in validating others, and that when you have something nice to say, go ahead and say it.

Wherever, Whenever

Lunch box notes can be delivered anytime and anyplace. The element of surprise will always be there if you are clever in choosing unexpected places to hide these secret missives. Every once in a while, leave a note for your child under her pillow as a nighttime reminder or bedtime prayer. Stick a note inside a schoolbook on the first day of school to provide a little encouragement in the classroom. Place a note in your child's toy box as a reminder to have fun and to tidy up! Whether it's found under the dinner plate on a special occasion or in the school box on a random Thursday, your lunch box letter will tell your children again and again that they are safe, that they belong, and that they are loved.

Gold Star

To encourage good behavior in your children, try reinforcing work well done in the permanence of ink. Give a thank-you note to your child; read it aloud at dinner and post it proudly on the refrigerator for the whole family to share.

Dear Dad

Sit down together and write Dad a note for his briefcase. Hide a note for Mom in her car. Reaching out to another family member in writing builds the kind of bond that even today's ten-hour workday can't break. If one parent consistently travels for work or carries a particularly busy agenda, writing notes with your child can keep that parent close at times of separation or stress, reminding the child of your constant presence despite prolonged periods of absence.

"A" Is for Appreciation

Looking for the perfect way to thank Miss Robson in Room 3A? Have your child express gratitude personally with a carefully crafted thank-you note this year. Schoolteachers across the United States are crying out in desperation that they simply have no more cupboard space required to accept even one more "I ♥ Teacher" coffee mug and no more drawer space to take on another worm-in-the-apple pencil sharpener.

Besides, it makes perfect sense that the teachers of America would rather see a child attempt letter writing than receive yet another oversized ceramic #2 pencil paperweight. Appreciate this country's educators with the gift they offered your child. Put your gratitude on paper. Better yet, ask your children to express it all on their own.

DON'T FORGET TO WRITE!

Separation in families is often an inevitable part of life. Certainly boarding school and summer camp present different challenges to children and their parents than death and divorce. But one theme, which we as adults tend to forget, is a constant: kids who are separated from their families over long periods of time for any reason—be it financial hardship or baseball camp—are going through a mildly traumatic experience. Babes at the breast begin life believing that separation from a parent is equivalent to death. Not surprisingly, children often operate unconsciously out of separation anxiety well into young adulthood or even longer.

Letter writing is a good way for families to stay connected when split apart by circumstances. Notes written from the heart of a loved one have the power to bring children home safe. So whether your kids are caught up in custody battles or in college classes, keep them close to your heart through the reassuring intimacy achieved by written correspondence.

DON'T ASK ME WHY

I never thought I'd grow up to be the kind of parent who, out of sheer exhaustion, relied upon the one phrase I'd detested most as a child: *"Why? Because I said so."* Believing I'd encourage my child's astounding innate curiosity, I was prepared to answer the whos, whats, wheres, and even the hows with precision and patience. But when *why* came along, increasing in its insistent frequency with each passing day, I fear I was woefully inept, not to mention painfully irritated. *Why* is a complicated crossword puzzle. You can't find the reason for *why* in the dictionary. And worst of all, *why* can only be answered a limited number of times with "Ask your father." Suffice it to say, the question *why* is a more laborious undertaking than I'd prefer to assume at 7:42 a.m. on Sunday morning before the mandatory family visit to church.

"Because I said so" is an enticing response for bedraggled parents to answer a child who has not yet reached an age when reasoning seems appropriate. (When exactly *is* that, by the way?) But it's also an empty response that leaves both child and parent feeling dissatisfied with its vapidity.

Children very often display an uncanny ability to grasp new concepts. Their capacity to comprehend the whys of life can be a source of constant amazement—if we attempt to satisfy their questions with real-life answers. *Why* is how we learn. So the next time you are tempted to summarily dismiss a parent's least-favorite question, take notice of the rare opportunity provided in this complex question. The child set upon discovery is like a wide-eyed fish intent upon the worm. Your response has the power to reel him in—or to lose his interest entirely.

So if you believe the notion that teaching your children letter writing is an invaluable endeavor that is worth the time and care required to teach it, you must be able to provide your children with satisfying answers regarding the *why* behind it. You will find over a dozen possible answers in "Building Blocks and Benefits" below.

Teaching your child the art of written correspondence will give birth to a rewarding lifelong pleasure that will benefit them professionally, socially, and psychologically.

Building Blocks and Benefits
The key to learning any discipline comes with the conscientious development of good habits. Because all of us learn at an early age to relate to the concept of building blocks, I found it appropriate to take that approach here. Read on and you will learn how to gradually lead your child into the practice of written correspondence. You will see some of the invaluable benefits they will reap in the process. Even better, you will be able to answer the *why* behind each invaluable life lesson. And finally, you will discover that written correspondence is a skill that has the power to create better people for a better world.

In Utero Habitualization Unborn babies begin to relate to the outside world through sensing sound vibration during the later stages of gestation. Unfortunately, it would be a stretch to imagine that a baby could somehow absorb writing etiquette simply because an expecting mother carefully scripts seventeen thank-you notes after the last round of baby gifts. Rather, the title of this section suggests that as a new parent, you are now the sole agent of your baby's early education.

Being a living example of personal values is to be your role from this day forth.

So if you've never given a thought to note writing in your life, you now have nine months to set this valuable practice in motion, building a habit worthy of passing on to your unborn child. Thankfully, pregnancy is an ideal time to get started—one filled with ample opportunities for gratitude. When a couple is expecting a baby, friends, family, neighbors, and even complete strangers rally around excitedly with lots of advice and opinions, gestures of kindness, and gifts of all kinds. Learn to express your appreciation by habitually acknowledging expressions of goodwill in writing. In this way, you will cultivate a practice that your child can emulate as he grows. Gratitude is a healthy outlet that communicates joy in the presence of new life. And taking the time to express that gratitude in writing fosters a feeling of family and community with those who celebrate beside you, one that can be passed down to the next generation.

The lesson? The attitude of gratitude is cultivated through habit.

Waxing Poetic Thankfully, children can first participate in the process of written correspondence without actually using words. In the early years, a parent may need to supply the written phrases included in a thank-you note, for example, but even a toddler can supplement sentiment by doodling. Before sending off the next thank-you note you've written on behalf of your child, encourage her participation in crayon. Or allow your children to express a bit of themselves in magic marker or colored pencil. I once received an envelope in the mail that had been decorated with bright flourishes of finger paint that stood out playfully among the dreaded monthly bills. Whether this form of "paper play" reveals a bright red handprint or an amoeba-like orb representing a human face, the recipient of your note will feel a small but unique connection with the child that is sure to provoke a smile.

The lesson? Paper is an outlet for self-expression.

ME-ism Primary socialization of children often comes with the violent shock that in order to get along in a group, one must begin thinking of others instead of solely the self. Interestingly enough, it would seem that a child's first awareness of others occurs when this other has something tangible to *offer*: "I know *you* by what you provide for *me*." Once a child begins to grasp the nature of this type of rapport, the "reception response," as I call it, is activated. This is the ideal time to learn the necessity of expressing gratitude in exchange—first verbally with a thank-you and then in writing. The written (or colorfully drawn) thank-you note is therefore the first logical step in teaching a child the importance of correspondence. Asking the child to take an active role in this exchange will guard him against an egocentric sense of entitlement and greed.

The lesson? Everyone owes someone a thank-you.

Noteworthy A girlfriend of mine once recalled for me the day her own habit of writing thank-you notes was formed. "When we were kids, Mom would not allow us to play with a new toy or gift *before* we wrote the thank-you note. It was always a race to see who would get to the mailbox and raise the flag first." To this day, my friend responds with sincerely expressed written gratitude immediately upon the reception of any gesture, card, or gift.

"The student who knows how to write will necessarily know how to think."

—John Merriman

When fostering the habit of writing notes, encourage your children to practice same-day responding. When a child is still excited about the gift, he is more likely to be enthusiastic about the task at hand and to readily express his joy to the giver.

The lesson? Thanks first.

Togetherness Is Key   In the case of the thank-you note, actively acknowledge the gift (or gesture) with an air of enthusiastic celebration and plenty of "wows!" Then help your children carefully choose the stationery that perfectly expresses their joy, or tap into the inner artist and create a unique handmade card with crayons, markers, stickers, glitter, or stencils. Guide them through the process of exploring the words or drawings to express themselves, walking through the rest of the mailing process together: "First we add the address (here), and then we put our stamp (right here), and then we walk the letter out to the mailbox. Don't forget to raise the flag. Here, I'll lift you up. We can watch for the mailman (usually he comes around noon or so), and when he arrives, he'll see our red flag, make a stop, and whisk our letter over to Aunt Colleen's house." With enough theatrical explanation and enthusiasm on your part, the children will be intrigued by this creative, artistic, and systematic ritual.

The lesson? Letter writing can be fun.

Just Because As your children become well versed in writing thank-you notes, they can begin to explore various other types of letter writing. Begin by encouraging them to choose a relative or friend at random and write a simple letter of greeting—just because. They can write to check in, to say hello, and to briefly describe what's new in their life. Suggest that they begin the note, for example, by explaining something about themselves—hobbies, likes and dislikes, subjects of interest in school—and then ask the same question of the letter's recipient. Writing letters simply for the purpose of making yourself known to another person and learning to know him as well is an exciting and intriguing process. When words are the only instrument of communication, friendship can grow in new and unique ways.

The lesson? Share—and grow.

Calling All Dads! I recently asked a male friend of mine to name the most crucial aspect of marketing his real estate business. He said, unequivocally, "writing thank-you notes." Contrary to the stereotype, writing notes and letters is not a "female practice," nor is it a superfluous hobby for especially creative housewives or a pastime for teenage schoolgirls bored by class lectures. Rather, written correspondence is an essential mode of communication for people in relationships of *any* kind—professional, social, romantic, or familial. In order to provide a good example for both boys and girls, encourage Dad to participate in the process of learning letter writing too.

The lesson? Communion with others is a universal human need.

Anytown, U.S.A. It's a big world out there. So much to see and explore. Encouraging young children to seek out a pen pal can provide endless life-enriching opportunities that extend far beyond one's own neighborhood. Establishing a relationship with a child of another state, another area of the country, or, indeed, another part of the world, can open up avenues of learning not available in the classroom. Pen pal relationships provide an intriguing, culturally enriching, and exciting rapport that gradually unfolds between two strangers with each sheet of paper written. And the letters received from foreign landscapes expose the recipient to worlds unknown—inciting curiosity and sharing knowledge about other people and various ways of life. In consciously seeking out others that exist outside a relatively small range of experience, children are granted the opportunity to learn that not all circumstances resemble their own. Not all people look, think, act, dress, or even talk like we do.

Often, a lifelong friendship is established between pen pals, creating further opportunities for travel—both in mind and in body. To the young pen pal, the letter becomes a gift through which one discovers intimacy in ink and the pleasure that arises through sharing one's self and being receptive to others.

In this cultural exchange of ideas, children inevitably discover the joy of giving and receiving, the pain of delayed gratification ("Is the mail here yet?!"), and the inevitable growth that stems from a mutually beneficial relationship. Through the exchange of letters, we learn valuable lessons: to take turns, to listen, and to share.

Pen pal relationships thrive without the impediments of initial bias, physical isolation, and financial limitation that may threaten to enclose us within the local sphere. Children are free to roam the world through loyally written, love-worn letters carried like open-ended tickets to a brightly beckoning world.

The lesson? Community extends beyond man-made borders.

Dear Diary Growing up sure isn't easy. As children grow into young adults, life inevitably becomes more complicated. The first real strains of communal living begin when a child enters school, develops relationships, and establishes his place in the classroom, which will be to a great extent the scope of his world for the next twelve years or so. As parents step out of the role of social referee, kids begin to represent themselves more fully, taking on the greater responsibility of expressing emotions in positive and socially acceptable ways. As we all know, this can be a frustrating process learned only through often painful, always rewarding practice.

Providing a child with his own diary gives a safe place where he can honestly and privately express feelings in a healthy way. The journal is a ready outlet for frustration, joy, confusion, anger, and excitement.

The lesson? Experiencing emotion is part of the human condition.

Journal writing also introduces children to the "self" in a very real way as they learn to transcribe its wondrous complexity on paper. This relationship with the self deepens as they learn to use this quietly effective tool to manage the inevitable twists and turns that occur throughout the growth process.

The lesson? Self-discovery is manifested in reviewing our thoughts, words, and behaviors.

One's private diary is a precious written collection of personal history that can be referred to in hindsight as a learning tool. As we plod forth through the challenges life presents, we are able to thus avoid repeated pitfalls and to learn the value of planning ahead for next time.

The lesson? We can learn from the past for a better future.

Provide your child with his or her own journal on a significant birthday or special occasion—perhaps a diary that locks with a special little key. Or keep it simple with a spiral-bound notebook that the child can easily hide under the bed or pillow. Impress upon your child that this is a private place where thoughts, feelings, and personal boundaries are sacred—a storehouse of secrets to be held close to the heart.

The lesson? Privacy is a human right.

Bedtime Basket Although as adults we are often nostalgic about the long-lost simplicity of childhood, we cannot deny that children can experience their own unique set of troubles. The challenges that children face are no less real to them than those their parents encounter, as all are experiencing these trials for the first time, which can be frightening at any age.

The Bedtime Basket is a safe and comforting outlet for childhood worries and a healthy habit to start at a young age. Provide your children with a small bedside basket and encourage them to write down the concerns that weigh heaviest on their heart, the resentments that they may have harbored during the school day, the hurt feelings they may suffer. The idea behind this notion is to unburden the child in order that he receives proper rest. Relieving the psyche each day of these unfortunate interruptions of good energy flow will allow your child a good night's sleep while providing peace and serenity at day's end.

The lesson? This too shall pass.

Santa Claus and Jesus We all need to be heard, to have our hopes and dreams recognized by an entity with the power to make us believe in something. Encourage your children to express their greatest desires on paper in the form of a letter to God—or Santa Claus. Although these two recipients merit a much different kind of correspondence, both are valid in their own way. Writing to Santa Claus is one of the fleeting but essential experiences of childhood. Without it, we may not know what it means to wish upon a star. Letters to God acknowledge the belief system that there exists a power greater than ourselves—a comforting presence to ensure we are never alone in this baffling and wonderful world.

The lesson? Wishes can come true.

Chicken Letters As a child I eagerly looked forward to going away to summer camp for the month of August. I remember with vivid recall the smell of the damp forest that surrounded our tiny wood cabins, the sound of the girlish laughter mixed with cricket song in the chilly night air, and the sweet exhilaration of passionate competition enjoyed in endless sporting activities. Among the memories I made while being away from home for the very first time, I will always remember one activity with a special fondness. Every Sunday at camp we were served a fried chicken dinner with

TV If kids are entertained by two letters, imagine the fun they'll have with twenty-six. Open your child's imagination.

all the buttery biscuits and mashed potatoes one could eat.
But in order to be awarded this delectable meal, we had to
write a weekly letter home to our parents, telling them of
our misadventures, of games and songs, of snake sightings,
ghost stories, and other delights. These became affectionately
known as "chicken letters," and I thank the camp counselors
to this day for providing me an outlet to reconnect with my
parents, who, whether or not I admitted it, I missed terribly.
Why not start your own unique letter-writing tradition at
your house? I would imagine the Chocolate Chip Cookie
Letter to be very popular.

The lesson? Relationships can survive periods of absence
if we keep in touch.

By teaching your children the art of written expression,
you will have given them the life skills required to know
and express themselves more fully, to appreciate others more
deeply, and to make a profound connection between the two.
Through writing, we learn to slow down a busy mind, to
pause and think, to consider our words, and to measure our
thoughts. The discipline you have fostered in your children
through this process will become the foundation for all of
their written endeavors—from term papers to love notes to
acceptance speeches.

The power of the written word is vast and alive. Does it
really have the might to create better people for a better
world? Decide for yourself . . .

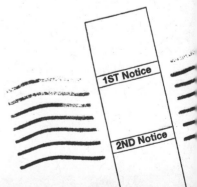

October 12, 1917

Dear Mother and Father

I am writing to you (rather messily, I fear) from the modern comfort of the dining car aboard the Taggart Transcontinental. I have twice spilled my coffee, so unaccustomed I am to this rickety mode of transportation. But you should see how she flies! I feel I am witnessing the very change of seasons racing past my window as we make our way across the vast patchwork quilt that is the Midwest. The farmhouses and fields are but a blur of faded autumn hues lit up by the fiery sunset of this fall afternoon.

The steady clicking rhythm beneath my feet is somehow soothing to me as my excitement grows. Here I am! Rapidly approaching my waiting future in the big city!

When I reach San Francisco, I shall first try to secure work, but will write you again at my first opportunity. I assure you that I will try to be home for the holidays, if the tickets aren't too dear.

Know that I am thinking of you as I begin this new adventure. I am eternally grateful for all you've done for me.

Your loving son,
John

OUR STORY

In preparation for writing this book, I asked my mother to
send me a box of old family letters written throughout the
early part of the last century. The letters themselves were
simple works of human art. I relished the feel of the yellowing,
tissue-thin paper and the way the faded ink had seeped deeply
into it, indelibly out of reach. I touched the curled edges of
ancient-looking postage stamps and noted their expired value
in mere pennies. And as I read the stories written in each of
the letters, I was swept away by the quaint verbal expressions
of older times, fascinated by the sweetly naive sentiments
expressed in writing, and intrigued by the societal norms
and personal histories that were revealed. I watched the slow
and steady development of ideas, invention, and inflation. I
witnessed in awe the pace, progress, politesse, and politics
of the generations who came before us. Though personally
unknown, these long-deceased characters seemed somehow
very familiar to me as kindred spirits with whom I share a
name and a bloodline. The tenuous spirit of an age gone by
rang through as clearly as if I'd been reading a newspaper
tossed enthusiastically in my lap by a 1932 paperboy.

As I read on, I was reminded of the vast distances that
often separated family, friends, and lovers long before the age
of technology brought the world to live within a computer
screen. The letters of this era spoke of a deep longing and
frustration due to the estrangement we no longer feel since
the advent of electronic mail. People of the day seemed to
work more conscientiously at keeping in touch with their
fellows, for they yearned for intimacy with loved ones
but lacked the modern conveniences we often take for

granted—access to automobiles, airplanes, and, of course, the Internet. The letters written during this period of time reveal a palpable desire to truly know one another in a way that we still long for today but no longer seem to achieve through more modern forms of communication.

As I explored these written archives further, I began to see the bigger picture of my own life through the lens of my family's history. I felt an unexpected and vague sadness that these people are no longer here on earth, and I began to wonder about their existence now. Could my deceased ancestors be watching me from a world beyond? I hoped so, and I was sparked with a sudden desire to make them proud of me and my somewhat quirky modern version of the family tradition.

As a second step in my book research, I excitedly unearthed an entire archive of personal letters I've both written and received over the years. Nestled within this simple cardboard box I discovered some truly priceless cargo. Among the wrinkled papers and torn envelopes I found a few juvenile declarations of love that made me laugh at my lack of maturity, letters from summer camp friends that brought up feelings of nostalgia for a former girlish self, notes of congratulations and encouragement from my parents that *still* make me feel ten feet tall, and a few explosive letters I'd written and (thankfully) never sent.

I then rediscovered multiple journals I had lovingly and loyally dedicated over the years. As I skimmed through pages filled with childhood joy and confusion, teenage angst and passion, and, finally, more adult issues ranging from self-image to faltering faith to romantic whims, I came to reacquaint myself with the girl I once was and to relive experiences that made me the woman I am today.

As I reread these treasures from my past, I was reminded of the valuable life lessons I'd learned, the places I'd seen, and the people with whom I'd shared parts of my life—some of whom I'd forgotten and others who remain with me now. While perusing this "photo album in words" and recalling the collection of my experiences, I was amazed by the tremendous growth I'd undergone in my short life here on earth and realized even more vividly my potential to grow into a brighter future.

I have no doubt that I will one day share some of these letters and journals with my children after I am gone, so that they may better know me and come to better know themselves, where they came from, and who they are.

Family writings resurrected from the past are a legacy to be passed down from generation to generation. Following are some practices you can begin with your children now to ensure that they will not miss out on the valuable lessons your family history has to teach them.

"Letters are among the most significant memorial a person can leave behind them."

—Johann Wolfgang von Goethe

A Box of "Who Am I?"

There is a shelf in my parents' home with six identical cardboard boxes, lined up all in a row. Each box has a white label with a name carefully stenciled by my young father for each of his six children. And I know well, when I visit my childhood home, that I am assured hours of nostalgic entertainment each time I remove this prized possession from its shelf.

Inside this dusty cardboard box lay the precious remnants of my life as a child: art projects made of clay and popsicle sticks, trophies, medals (a few of the "honorable mentions" we so dreaded), report cards, photographs of happy children showing faces smeared with chocolate birthday cake, ribbons from spelling bees, and, of course, all of the letters, essays, stories, and notes I wrote during the course of my childhood.

Begin an archive for each of your children and fill it with the artifacts of their lives. Encourage your kids to participate in creating this treasure trove by saving their own letters, cards, school essays, and significant journal entries. They'll thank you when they visit home one day with their *own* children.

Dear Descendants

In Marilynn Robinson's novel *Gilead*, we are privy to a sequence of letters written from an elderly father to his young son—a sort of life manual passed from one generation to the next. Because this aging father believes he is soon to die of a weary heart, he dedicates this memoir to his son, telling him of all the things he may not have time to say before he departs this world. He speaks to his son as an adult, knowing that the child will likely read this diary many years in the future, and tells him vivid stories of how their family came to be, detailing its place in time among the many colorful characters of their small midwestern town. Although few of us will likely dedicate an entire book of letters to our children, we can each attempt a note or two, describing a seemingly mundane circumstance to be cherished and not forgotten.

If you were to write such a letter to your child, what would you tell him?

I am looking out the window from my second-story office and watching you play with your friend Tony in the sprinklers. You are wearing your red swim trunks, and your pale, taut little six-year-old body seems sculpted of only muscle and bone. The spring sun is not yet strong enough to keep you warm, but the two of you insisted on imitating an Indian rain dance you saw on television last night. The water must be as cold as ice as it shoots rainbows into the late-morning sky, and the sounds of your delightful squeals make the corners of my mouth turn up in a soft and knowing smile. I could watch you play forever and ever . . .

Record Book
We've all been regaled by the incredible things that children say in their younger years. Wisdom that seems far beyond their age suddenly bursts forth in sometimes omniscient, other times naive statements that beg not to be forgotten. Try keeping a diary of your child's quotations throughout those formative years by placing a notebook near the phone with a pencil at the ready to record the funny things your kids say. What better gift to give them when they go off to college?

We had been decorating the tree all morning and the house was a disaster of broken ornaments, tinsel, and tangled Christmas lights. When I looked up from stuffing a cardboard box full of wrinkled red tissue paper, there you were, standing by the fireplace with the cloth arm cover of our family room couch over your head like a miniature shepherd. "I'm going to Buffalo Ham," you said.

Postcards from the Past

Just after college graduation, I lived in France for almost three years. Thankfully, I thrived amidst the homesickness I experienced living in a foreign country "grace à la" constant stimulation of learning another people, language, and culture. To stay connected with family and friends back home, I also wrote and received a lot of letters. And each time I wrote a letter or postcard, I would ask the recipient to carefully set it safely aside for my return. And now, better than any photo album I could ever hope for, I have a written essay of my adventures in Europe as seen through my eyes and expressed to the people I love. I cherish these memoirs so much that I have repeated this practice again and again—asking those to whom I write to save the letters I send from various destinations, trips, vacations, and retreats. Sometimes in the long run the letters have more value to me as the writer than they do the recipient.

Story Time

If you happen to be in possession of letters or journal entries taken from your family history, share them with your children as bedtime stories. Children love to hear about the first time you met your future spouse, or stories describing the life you lived as a child. They will ask you again and again to retell the story of their birth, vividly detailing the exciting day that led up to the cataclysmic moment when a new life came to arrive on this earth. True life stories are enriching and allow your children to better know who you are, as a separate and unique individual with a past full of memories worthy of sharing.

Recognizing the past in inked reality gently introduces children to the idea of mortality. By being exposed to your family history, they will learn that living things are fleeting, that life does not go on forever, that nothing material is permanent. Wallpaper fades, families move, traditions are lost, heirlooms misplaced, and details forgotten. But with every ending, there is comfort to be found in memory; for while it's true that our loved ones might not be with us forever, the endurance of the human spirit is everlasting and it lives on in our hearts.

Time passes by so quickly. Let's not waste a single moment.

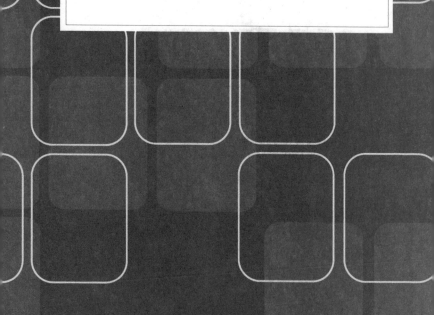

Although there are no hard and fast rules, the following principle applies: certain communications call for a simple distribution of information; others demand a more intimate exchange.

E-mail

I once considered myself a purist—the kind of "classic communicator" who would always prefer engraved papers, fountain pens, and wax seals as the hallmarks of my carefully crafted correspondence. I've always enjoyed the tactile sensation, the ritual, the sheer romance of the written letter; I never considered there may come a day when letter writing might be viewed as an outdated mode of communication. And then e-mail came along . . .

This technological marvel presented an amazing new form of instantaneous communication that promised to eliminate the need for previously basic necessities of written correspondence—pen, paper, postage, and (most of all) patience! Although the devout pen pal in me was instantly intrigued by the convenience of this newfangled method for keeping in touch, I initially refused to investigate further, condemning the idea of "electronic" communication as impersonal. (Humph!)

While it seemed entirely possible that *information* could be propelled speedily down this bizarre new rabbit hole, I feared that *sentiment* would not survive such a tumultuous journey. I imagined that all emotion would be violently stripped from our words as they were crammed into the narrowing tunnels of a chilly cyberspace.

Would this new invention unite our world in previously unseen ways, or would it serve to unwittingly scatter us further in a dangerous trend of technologically imposed isolation? In a society of people who already found themselves removed from the intimacy that high-tech seemed destined to abolish, computers were fast becoming our *primary connection* to the outside world. The potential loss of life-sustaining community posed by the death of the handwritten letter made me shiver. It seemed somehow tragic to witness the slow decay of the thread that had once tied us together so beautifully and so very personally since the first wing-footed messenger was dispatched across the plains.

And so I refused to jump on this futuristic bandwagon in the same way I had dismissed other technological upgrades, believing it was a trend that would climax and fade. How wrong I was.

E-mail was not a fad that would come and go like some fleeting case of high-tech hiccups. Rather, it was a force destined to take over modern communication as we knew it. It was not long before the entire world began operating almost solely through electronic channels. Nor would it be much longer before staunch resistors like me would become completely excluded from the proverbial inner circle.

I had a choice: I could either continue to cling to my dwindling belief that paper, pen, and phone calls were the only tools that offered the possibility of worthy human connection, or I could just give a mental shrug, log on, and adapt to this innovative mode of communication with the same enthusiasm I'd holstered my beloved cell phone.

These days I admit to being a chronic e-mailer. I not only take advantage of the convenience and speed that keep me closely connected with professional contacts, family, and friends across the globe, but I find the witty, rapid-fire repartee of e-mail to be a source of joy and laughter throughout my day. You might say I've sold out; but the fact is, I am still truly a pen pal at heart. You won't soon find me giving up my love-softened leather-bound journal or hear me refer to postal letters as "snail mail." I will always take great pleasure in writing the now-considered antiquated letter for my more personal correspondence.

But after many years of successfully navigating both cyberspace and the vast universe of the blank page, I see that to skillfully alternate between these two mediums is a wonderful way to enjoy the best of both worlds. Both methods of soliloquy have their proper place in correspondence, whether we choose the immediate exchange of information achieved through e-mail or the sentimental intimacy shared by poets of the written word.

Letter writers, keyboard kings, and professional correspondents *can* have it all. There is clearly a place for e-mail in contemporary communication, and there are certain occasions that call for the handwritten note as well. And as with so many of the tools we have at our disposal today, mastering the nuances between these two modes of communication can maximize the impact of the method we choose. The secret is learning when to relinquish the keyboard and resurrect the stationery. This next section will make that decision easier.

DECISIONS, DECISIONS

The determining factor in choosing between the keyboard and the pen is not made along the crooked little line that divides personal and professional correspondence. After all, many of us keep up with personal contacts via e-mail as well as write the odd note to a colleague at work.

When choosing the proper medium to make contact with another person, it is important to recognize whether the correspondence conveys information or intimacy. While e-mail is the perfect medium to communicate fact, the handwritten note is a superior means to express feelings.

The Daily News

One of e-mail's most immediately gratifying qualities is its ability to instantaneously connect us with loved ones separated by any span of distance on a daily (or even hourly) basis. Be it across the country or across the ocean, no other form of rapid-fire communication can sustain relationships so well or satisfy our eagerness so deeply for the news *du jour*. Keeping in touch with family and friends would likely not be possible without such a convenient and economically facile medium. Sending news of seemingly trivial miscellanea can bring loved ones closer to the daily life experiences that might not merit a lengthy phone call but surely call out for a quick instant message before beginning dinner preparations.

Although often brief and impetuous, e-mail has the ability to truly unify the estranged when tempered with sensitivity. A quick click of the mouse enables instant "conversation." What could be better?

The Need for Speed
E-mail is a world without the wait. And in modern-day business, when information can be transferred faster than the speed of human thought, a lengthy pause can mean the difference between success and disaster. That's why when it absolutely positively has to be there NOW, e-mail is the way to go. Out of the office? Fear not. Incredibly, the BlackBerry handheld computer allows those who must be mobile to remain connected throughout the day.

Unfortunately, this frenetic quest for speed too often sacrifices the consideration and care we would normally take to safeguard our communications against potential misunderstanding and embarrassment. The next section of this chapter explains how to maintain responsible e-mail correspondence. Suffice to say for now that proofreading is a must. While we often trust our computers to eliminate spelling and grammatical errors, there is no substitute for the mind's eye and its ability to carefully avoid inappropriate phrasing or content. When it's crucial, be careful not to assume that every sent message has been read or even viewed. Always follow up on truly urgent issues by telephone to call attention to your e-mail message.

Documentation
If ever you're in doubt about what he said, she said, or *you* said, just scroll down.

"If you tell the truth, you don't have to remember anything."

—Mark Twain

With the proper e-mail settings, each message sent and received conveniently contains every previous comment exchanged on that particular subject. Like a built-in court reporter, e-mail can provide a written transcript of our words, whether we like it or not. So the next time documentation is required to "CYA," you won't have to feel like a hospital patient in a backless paper gown with nowhere to hide a recording device.

But with advancement comes responsibility. Having our own words presented back to us can be a humiliating experience. Consider your dialogue with great care, despite the frenzied pace of the modern workplace. Allow yourself ample time to choose statements that express your ideas with tact, respect, and, of course, proper spelling.

Long Distance

Prime opportunities for satisfying and lucrative employment may not always exist in one's own neighborhood. Talented and dedicated employees are often presented with interesting prospects that involve extensive travel or even relocation. When blessed with a family at home, it's a tough choice. But if this once-in-a-lifetime opportunity calls for a temporary separation, e-mail can serve as a ready remedy for heartache. Electronic correspondence is available anytime and almost anyplace. So when it's almost midnight in London and your slumbering stateside partner won't be disturbed, a "missing you" message will be waiting patiently when she wakes.

The Late Show

It's Sunday morning. As you turn the page on your day-timer, you almost spill your coffee upon discovering that today's her birthday. You can't very well sneak out of the house to shop. Where do you go?

When the world is "out of the office" and there is no one to call, we can conveniently get our needs met on the Internet: Google-searching for the right point of reference, buying a gift online, researching a topic, looking up a telephone number. Through electronic mail, you can order patio furniture in winter, do your taxes on April 14, or make contact with a friend overseas in the wee hours of the morning.

Perhaps your mental ticker works best at night. Maybe you're an early riser. Whenever it is that your brain juices are fluidly flowing, e-mail is there to accommodate any need you might have without forcing you to lob a rude awakening upon those who don't share your particular circadian rhythm. And once that crucial piece of late-night information is placed gingerly in another's e-mailbox, you can relax and tiptoe off to bed, knowing that—thanks to e-mail—this one little tidbit will not be lost or forgotten, nor will it keep you from a good night's sleep.

Schizophrenic Soccer Mom

Many of us find ourselves acting out a variety of life roles throughout the course of a single day. At a morning meeting, we might be an opinionated and articulate committee chairman, only to be reduced to babbling baby talk upon encountering a certain one-year-old at lunch. Before choosing the proper mode of correspondence for a particular situation, an appropriate question to ask yourself is, "Who is this correspondence *from*?" From YOU, of course! It may sound silly. But *which* of your personas do you wish to portray in this instance? You are likely a complex creature who ably fills multiple shoes simultaneously. Are you writing as a business associate or as a family friend, as a mother or as a vice president? Electronic mail clearly and appropriately communicates a business concern, while letter mail eloquently reveals the human being behind the persona. Which of your "multiple personalities" is speaking at present?

Office Etiquette

If a flimsy particleboard wall is all that serves to distinguish you from a colleague in the next cubicle, individuality risks getting lost in the maze. Adding personality to your office persona provides a sweet sort of freedom from the shackles of the daily grind. How to separate your unique self from the masses? Put it in writing. In our penchant for productivity, we tend to relegate all office correspondence to the annals of e-mail. But consider for a moment the profound impact of a handwritten note on a weary and wrinkled colleague. In an environment of competition, judgment, and high expectation, periodic notes of appreciation and encouragement are desperately needed to oil the overworked machine of the human heart. Your missive might take the form of congratulatory applause after a promotion or a simple pat on the back for a point well made. Follow the close cousin to your mother's advice: if you have something nice to say, go ahead and say it.

What could be classier or more professional and considerate than an executive who takes time out of his busy schedule to handwrite a note to a subordinate? Investing in some *personal* stationery for your *professional* correspondence separates the individual from the firm, making a boldly sincere statement about the person behind the post. Not "from the desk of . . ." but from the heart.

He Loves Me, He Loves Me . . . *What?*
The day I received my first wedding e-vite, I could have cried. I envisioned Don McLean's tune about "the day the music died" being sung in place of the wedding march.

Because wedding invitations have loyally adhered to the more traditional side of etiquette and decorum, they boast a presentation that remains in the elegant tradition of a more romantic time. Nuptial announcements are among the most beautiful, the most eloquent, and the most sophisticated kind of communication by mail. Such delicately packaged paper delights are a celebration in and of themselves, inciting an anticipation that aptly announces the coming of a great event. Thickly lined envelopes, gossamer tissue, creamy cotton paper, curling organza ribbon, and carefully engraved calligraphy convey the heartfelt excitement of the upcoming affair as splendidly as Pachelbel's Canon. Electronic invitations seem a weak substitute whose effect in bearing such momentous news is most anticlimactic.

Love letters, wedding announcements, bold declarations of affection, and *certainly* wedding invitations deserve nothing less than to be committed to paper and sent by the same careful ring-bearing hand that extends these romantic gestures.

Tragically, rumors abound describing a monstrous entity bound and set upon killing the last vestiges of romance. Known as the E-PROPOSAL, this unwholesome breach of etiquette is often mistaken for a genuine declaration of love. One can only hope that these are the makings of urban myth! Do not be fooled: the kind of man who proposes marriage through e-mail is the sort who would send his *brother* to help you pant through a Lamaze class.

Outstanding

I once heard it theorized that modern man is exposed to more information in one day than our Victorian ancestors encountered in an entire lifetime. That thought alone could cause a person to feel, shall we say, overstimulated.

Personal e-mail, business e-mail, electronic memos, instant messages—how can the average person possibly file it all neatly away within the mental confines of our wee human brains? Fired with a speed beyond comprehension, one piece of information seems to blend furtively into the next or simply gets lost in the shuffle.

How exactly can we ensure that a particular piece of correspondence is actually retracted from a heavily stacked inbox as it tilts precariously over capacity in cyberspace?

When applying for a job, it is a French tradition to handwrite letters of intent to accompany your resume. Perhaps it is believed that a person's handwriting is indicative of the person *behind the paper*. Indeed, what better way to call attention to your correspondence than to send it in your own unique writing, using color, shape, texture, and the tactile scent and sensation of real paper.

And although your note may not be preceded by that often annoying little electronic bong that announces the presence of "new mail," the sheer substance of a real three-dimensional letter has the power to virtually leap forth from the mental monitor in a way no flat and lifeless e-mail can. Unlike exposure to the constant scrolling gyrations of a computer screen, a person with a card or letter in hand is attentive, focused, and single-minded. If it's a response you desire, there is no better method to reach out and seize this captive attention.

Spunk Mail

Keeping our long-term relationships fresh and interesting often calls for a little extra effort to keep complacency at bay. Whether it's a pen pal, a childhood friend, or the love of your life, open channels of communication keep relationships alive. A healthy rapport sustains itself by drawing from many forms of communion—mind and body, heart and soul. Relying solely on limited modes of communication can stifle the potential we have to truly know another person, sacrificing the intimacy we seek.

Familiarity rejoices in the unexpected. Add a refreshing dose of surprise to your relationships and you may witness barriers to closeness melting, walls of resistance cracking, a shaft of sunlight penetrating the shadows of boredom to reveal a smirk of pleasure, a heartfelt smile, or a ripple of laughter. The creatively terse spunk of a well-composed e-mail, the spontaneity of an unexpected phone call, the element of secrecy and surprise in the instant message, the soothing handclasp of the written letter—all should blend together to create a whole picture of this wonderful being we've chosen to know.

Unfortunately, in this modern world of tumultuous trends and fantastical fads, we tend to forget the place from whence we came. Fatigued by the demanding "convenience" of high-speed exchanges, we often neglect communication in its previous, more primitive forms. If written correspondence remains an untapped source of intimacy in your life, perhaps it's time to consider the unifying power of a lunch box letter, a thank-you note, or a carefully composed love letter—gestures of written support conveying true human sentiments from congratulations to condolences.

Today's world offers a myriad of ways to reach out to others—all within easy grasp of our fingertips. It would be a shame to neglect the intriguing possibilities.

Junk Mail

I am fortunate to live in a small mountain town—the kind of town where a visit to the post office is a truly social affair. I've never seen a mailman walking the streets here. The mail doesn't come to us; we go to the mail. And at least three times a week, I walk along the carefully maintained bike path to the post office. I chat it up with Darlene behind the counter, who's always quick with a smile and the weather report. Darlene knows my name and my box number, and often favors me with access to my mailbox even if I've forgotten my key. It makes me feel special.

In order to lighten my load for the trip back home, I sift through my stack of mail and promptly pitch what we affectionately call "junk mail," which usually makes up more than half the kitty. During this time, I observe the other visitors as they work through their own piles. I notice we have a very similar ritual. And from what I can tell, people don't much like getting their mail. But just imagine this scenario:

With a weary hand, she worries through the dreaded load of bills and circulars that habitually plague her small metal portal to the world. And into the garbage can, one wasted tree after another, sails the junk mail. Plunk ... plunk ... (slight hesitation) ... plunk. Every so often, a hint of curiosity sneaks across the sifter's face, like a hunkering prospector intently peering into the rushing waters of an old river, searching for gold. A brightly colored envelope is released from the stack and brought slowly to her face for closer investigation. A sort of questioning wonderment appears. "For ... me? From ... who?" Ah! A spark of recognition and delight, a quiet smirk—she cautiously looks both ways to keep the secret safe. Familiar handwriting or a specific postmark serve as clues to reveal the mystery. And her face is splashed with cold-water joy at the realization of the discovery's value. "For me ... From you!" The envelope is quickly slashed open then and there, its contents devoured with eyes as speedy as a hungry child's. Or perhaps she carefully places this small treasure on the stack of "keepers" and rushes back into the spring air, intent upon freeing the jewel from its traveling container with grandmother's antique letter opener and savoring every word over a cup of her favorite tea.

And yet when it comes time to respond to this "gift in paper," what will she do? Will she respond in kind, or will she resort to the habitudes of so many busy people? She might plop down heavily in front of the computer, check her bank account balances online, delete more unwanted junk mail, pay her bills, and, fatigued at the thought of her ever-increasing poverty, she may simply set the once-cherished postal missive aside and get up from the computer to hook up a coffee IV.

Finally, when all of her online busyness is taken care of, she shoots a quick e-response back to her dear pen pal friend before bolting off to work.

No time to bother with salutations, responses, or even the slightest consideration, she hastily types: "Got your letter. Thanx alot!" She pauses—the response seems somehow terse and insensitive when compared to her recent joy at the post office, so as an afterthought, to cauterize her laziness, she adds one of these symbols: :) Cute.

Boooooo! Hissssss! Never ever . . . *(ever!)* respond to a handwritten letter via e-mail! This is a total "thumbs down" in the world of correspondence etiquette. Consider the mannerless message you are sending to the dear person who took the valuable time to address you personally with paper and pen: "I wish you had been there to see the unfettered joy and gratitude with which I encountered your wonderfully unexpected letter. And what beautiful stationery! Your carefully scripted note reminded me that despite our estrangement, you still care about me and our long-standing friendship. How touching. Unfortunately, I won't be showing you the same consideration. I'm much too busy for you. Take this e-mail as a token of my disdain." Ouch!

Time Crunch
We are all busy people. Or more likely, we all *think* we are busy people. But before blindly accepting that your hectic, frantic, and, more accurately—over-scheduled—lifestyle doesn't allow the requisite time for paper correspondence,

carefully consider the time involved in writing a letter. Let's be realistic: how much time does it really take to put pen to paper? Fear not. Considering the demands of my busy reader's schedule, I've taken the liberty of timing this process.

Stationery selection: fifteen seconds
Writing thank-you note: three minutes
Addressing: eleven seconds
Applying stamp: three seconds

In under five precious minutes, you can extend the genuine hand of gratitude to someone who undoubtedly deserves your appreciation.

The secret to quick correspondence is not only to keep enticing personal stationery, postage stamps, and an address book within easy reach but to practice! Through habitual repetition, we become well-versed in the simple language of written discourse, which becomes more comfortable and sincere as we practice.

Too Close to Home

While it may often be readily accepted (and indeed necessary for documentation purposes) to send your coworker an e-mail in the cubicle next door, try to stay away from the habit of electronic correspondence at home. Sending an e-mail or instant message to your wife, husband, or child down the hall is lazy, unnecessary, and chillingly distant. A teenager who responds mechanically from the cave of his bedroom to the digitally expressed "Dinner's ready" likely won't have much to say at the table. In the same way, receiving a message late one night in the den from your wife about coming to bed is not nearly as enticing as soft fingertips on the neck and a whisper in the ear.

Gratitude Schmattitude
No doubt, at one point or another, you have been the resentful recipient of a painfully perfunctory e-mail in response to your expensive and carefully selected gift. You may have longed to respond to this abbreviated and insulting "confirm receipt" by asking, "Did you lose your manners or just your mind?" This failed attempt at forced gratitude may very well cause you to reconsider the next time a certain someone's birthday rolls around . . .

Reconciliation
The value we place on friendship is directly proportionate to the time we are willing to spend on its cultivation. When problems crop up between friends, and an apology is required to successfully move ahead, reconciliation is simply too important to be relegated to the brevity of e-mail in hopes of a quick fix. In situations that call for delicacy and decorum, many an abbreviated instant message has been wholly misinterpreted, only to fuel a more volatile argument than was started with. *Touchy* subjects require a more *personal touch*. How many misunderstandings have been caused by messages delivered all too swiftly in clipped e-mail sent by the cyber savvy? Instead, avoid unnecessary secondary arguments by keeping reconciliation friendly with a well-written repair.

DEAD LETTER OFFICE?

You've reached the final chapter of a manuscript dedicated almost entirely to heralding the value of written correspondence—a personal statement that has attempted to present the romantic, historic, and therapeutic benefits of putting pen to paper. Perhaps many of you have come to share the opinion expressed in this book—that practicing written communication has the power to deepen intimate relationships, decrease stress levels, foster gratitude, increase self-esteem, promote social harmony, teach life-coping skills, and improve emotional well-being. Others may not choose to embrace this theory in its entirety but will hopefully write the occasional thank-you note simply by code of etiquette, or perhaps keep a diary in pursuit of self-discovery.

I remain more convinced than ever that writing is an undeniably worthy practice that should be carefully preserved in this technologically advancing age. However, though idealistic, I am no fool. I realize that, due to the sheer convenience and unmatched speed of e-mail, electronic communication will likely remain a thread permanently enmeshed in our social fabric. I am also aware that even for those who agree wholeheartedly with the *notion* of written correspondence, the discipline to follow through in practice may comprise a more difficult promise.

For although we might long for greater intimacy in our relationships, although we have tremendous admiration for practitioners of the written word, although we take enormous pleasure in discovering a rare and unexpected personal letter among a stack of bills, we simply lack the patience to participate in this practice ourselves. In a society accustomed to instant gratification, we are less inclined to invest the requisite time in either the creation or the delivery of a handwritten note. Sigh . . .

Have we therefore come to a bitter end in the tale of letter mail? Hardly. There will always be those romantics among us who will cling loyally to our leather-bound journals, thrill at the prospect of a new fountain pen, and collect beautiful paper from all over the world in anticipation of the perfectly penned note. But for the mouse-and-keyboard crowd who readily admit their e-mail addiction, I respectfully refrain from judgment. Although the modern medium of choice may be electronic, the message can remain meaningful. It is wholly possible to enjoy the immediacy of instant correspondence without sacrificing soul. These basic guidelines of e-mail etiquette will show you how to keep your keyboard communications polite and personal.

Mass Appeal

E-mail is a highly practical way to reach a mass audience instantaneously. This is incredibly useful when communicating critical news to a large group of contacts in times of celebration or crisis. Beyond time savings alone, the advantages are many: comfort and support are returned to the sender en masse without the interruption of untimely phone calls; concerned friends and family feel important and included in the situation and can be unobtrusively heard; group updates can easily be added as relevant information comes to light.

When using e-mail to approach a group of people, whether to communicate tragedy or special occasion, it is best to use the "blind copy" feature to at least *pretend* that each individual is personally addressed, rather than being lumped together in a seemingly meaningless swarm. When writing mass e-mail, I typically send the original document to myself, placing the others on my list discreetly in the blind copy section. In this way, each individual sees only his or her name on the message and does not trouble over whoever else may be on your list of preferred recipients.

Great Salutations

Because the e-mail template conveniently provides us with many of the necessary components originally used in the letter-writing format—automatically citing the sender, recipient, subject, date, and time—we have relinquished the human warmth formerly communicated through more traditional ways of greeting one another. The best way to ensure a more personal touch in your electronic correspondence is to type the message in letter form. Begin with a salutation such as "Dear So and So," rather than skipping this small piece of etiquette as unnecessary. An e-mail that begins with a simple "hello," rather than diving straight into its subject matter, is immediately more personal and well received.

Dirty Little Secret

Although the blind copy feature on your e-mail can be quite useful to make an individual feel personally addressed amidst a large group, it can also get you into a world of trouble when its intention is exclusionary. In modern businesses that exist almost exclusively on e-mail, some companies discourage or even forbid its use altogether. Be wary of allowing an anonymous third party to "spy" on your communications. Clandestine correspondence smacks of unprofessional dishonesty and is the e-mail equivalent to whispering behind someone's back. When the whole picture is eventually and inevitably developed, it's unsightly to discover the belated appearance of two fingers poised menacingly above one's head.

Personality Is the Point

In the average seventy-five-plus e-mail day, every cyber message that pops up on the screen begins to look alike. How boring. This unfortunate redundancy tends to make e-mail blend together into an unrecognizable information overload, which often leads to an itchy trigger finger poised just above "delete."

One way to insure that your correspondence will stand out is the addition of a little personality. E-mail conveniently provides for uniqueness in our messages through the use of templates. Try setting one up for your personal correspondence that incorporates a more script-like (yet legible) font. Change the color of your lettering to a bolder hue, or up the font size for unmistakable clarity. Use one of the many stylish stationeries offered to add a decorative wallpaper behind your words. Add your own unique signature or an inspirational quote of the week designed to convey your personal style and credo.

(NOTE: In business correspondence, it's best to keep things simple. While font and color changes are encouraged to eliminate monotony in personal correspondence, multiple additions such as wallpaper can clog the cyber pipeline with data-dense messages, resulting in painfully slow transfer.)

Garbage Disposal

For some illogical reason, e-mail is considered by some to be a highly disposable form of communication. Perhaps within the tangible limits of the human mind, an electronic message seems to disappear immaterially into cyberspace without a trace once we push the send button. In reality, nothing could be farther from the truth. And so we risk a tendency to carelessly fling our words into this technological whirligig to be quickly transferred and subsequently forgotten. While in the immediate it may seem that no tactile paper proof of a particular line of correspondence exists, one can easily be produced and "admitted into evidence" at any point in the future. The file cabinets of an e-mail server are endless catacombs where information can ultimately be retrieved with the click of a mouse. Although we may have the illusion that we are sitting behind some sort of weighty velvet curtain when smugly snuggled behind our home computer, there is no such thing as an anonymous author. The electronic trail of bread crumbs is never lost, even when we believe we are achieving permanent deletion by relegating our regrettable dialogue to the trash can. Conscientious communication means never having to worry that our words, once typed, will last forever.

DELETE OR SAVE

When electronic mail first emerged as the latest technological wonder, e-mail instantly dominated the world of business, greatly reducing copier, fax, and general paper use.

A little more gradually, e-mail then became the preferred mode of communication to maintain *social* contacts as well. Close friends who once enjoyed staying close through personal letters and phone calls drastically abbreviated their

- *Name game.*
  In the body of your e-mail, refer to the recipient by name to
  ensure a more conversational tone.

  > I'm a little perplexed by this, Carl, and I'm hoping you
  > can enlighten me.

- *2 cute!*
  Refrain from using e-mail shorthand such as "BTW" in
  the place of "by the way," or any other forms of abbreviated
  electronic language.

  > C U @ the party!

- *No need to shout!*
  Using all capital letters to convey urgency may be perceived
  as rude and bossy. Use gentler italics instead.

  > Please respond *before* 10:00 a.m. with your decision on
  > this subject.

- *Poetic license.*
  Unless you fancy yourself something of an evolving
  E. E. Cummings, it's best to use proper capitalization in
  our typed communications. Although Mr. Cummings
  successfully pulled off this unique style of writing in his
  celebrated poetry, the rest of us may seem simply illiterate.

  > please send a contact name asap, time being of the
  > utmost importance. will send tomorrow by fedex.